5/13   £s   (206)

C000092239

IMAGES 35

Best of British Illustration 2011

AOI
Association
of illustrators

Images 35

Published by
The Association of Illustrators
2nd Floor, Back Building
150 Curtain Road
London EC2A 3AT
Tel. +44 (0)20 7613 4328
Fax +44 (0)20 7613 4417
info@theaoi.com
theAOI.com
AOIimages.com

ISBN 978-0-9558076-6-4

Production in Hong Kong by
Hong Kong Graphics and Printing Ltd
Tel: (852) 2976 0289
Fax: (852) 2976 0292

The Association of Illustrators

AOI Board of Directors
Beach, Ramón Blomfield,
Paul Bowman, Andrew Coningsby,
Rod Hunt

AOI Chair
Rod Hunt

AOI Deputy Chair
Beach

AOI Images Committee
Ramón Blomfield, Adam Graff,
Rod Hunt, Sabine Reimer,
Helen Thomas

Advisers
Stephanie Alexander, Ronan Deazley,
Tony Healey, Christine Jopling,
Robert Lands, Alison Lang,
Samantha Lewis, Fig Taylor,
Anna Vernon, Bee Willey

Managing Director
Ramón Blomfield
ramon@theaoi.com

Projects Manager
Derek Brazell
derek@theaoi.com

Images Co-ordinator
Sabine Reimer
images@theaoi.com

Events and Exhibitions Manager
Helen Thomas
events@theaoi.com

Membership Co-ordinator
Paul Ryding
info@theaoi.com

Finance Manager
Rasheed Musa
finance@theaoi.com

Book Design
Simon Sharville
simonsharville.co.uk

Patrons

Glen Baxter
Peter Blake
Quentin Blake
Raymond Briggs
Chloe Cheese
Carolyn Gowdy
Brian Grimwood
John Hegarty
David Hughes
Shirley Hughes
Sue Huntley
Mick Inkpen
Donna Muir
Ian Pollock
Gary Powell
Tony Ross
Ronald Searle
Paul Slater
Ralph Steadman
Peter Till
Janet Woolley

Contents • • • • • • • • • • • • • • • • • • •

Welcome to Images 35, the best of British Illustration 2011

Rod Hunt • AOI Chairman

Rod Hunt is a London based illustrator who has built a reputation for retro tinged illustrations and detailed character filled landscapes for UK and international clients spanning publishing, design, advertising and new media, for everything from book covers to advertising campaigns, theme park maps and even the odd large scale installation too!

Rod is also the artist behind the bestselling books 'Where's Stig?' and 'Where's Stig? The World Tour' for the BBC's hit TV show Top Gear.

Images, Britain's most prestigious illustration competition reaches its 35th year showcasing the very best talent that British illustration has to offer. Our industry has changed considerably in that time, not least due to the development of technology and media considered science fiction back in 1976 when the first Images book was published. The World Wide Web changed everything in little over a decade, and the iPad is moving content on again. No doubt illustration will evolve still further in keeping with the times.

Images has also developed in the last thirty-five years – the first Images book was printed in glorious monotone. Although reassuringly, some things haven't changed – both Brian Grimwood and Ian Pollock were in the first Images book and today they both appear in Images 35. I find it heartening that illustrators can sustain a career for nearly four decades and still be producing high quality, relevant and award winning work.

In some ways, certain things seem to have come full circle. Thirty-five years ago the UK economy was

going through difficult times, just as today's economic outlook is again uncertain. Nevertheless, we can take heart that illustration talent continues to set creative standards in a crowded marketplace despite economic difficulty. Images continues to be a quality resource for clients to access world class illustrators for their projects, and its strength lies in the work having been selected by industry professionals, the people who know illustration best, those who actually make and commission it. The judges have a difficult task and I thank them for discharging this responsibility with such commitment.

It's also worth highlighting that British illustrators' talent and creativity is respected and in demand the world over. Their work is a huge export, a notable contribution to the UK economy – Government, please take note of the value to the UK economy when passing copyright legislation, legislation, which does not act in the interest of the creators. Illustrators' rights need to be protective to ensure that creators receive the rewards they are entitled to.

What of the next generation? Young British illustrators getting their first taste of industry recognition in the New Talent Refresh Award? Inclusion in Images 35 provides a platform to give them confidence that their talent can spur them forward and that with commitment they can enjoy rewarding illustration careers. When studying for my Degree, I remember looking through past copies of Images in the college library and thinking that I wanted to be like the illustrators in the book, a real illustrator. At the time I lacked the confidence to enter. Today's new entrants, these newly recognised **professional** illustrators already have a head start on many others.

As we admire the work on the pages of Images 35 and congratulate this year's winners – everyone featured in this book – we can be sure that the work showcased here is by today's leading lights and richly deserving the spotlight.

1976

1977

1981

1982

1985

1992

1995

1997

Foreword
Ian Pollock • Illustrator

Born in 1950 in Macclesfield, Cheshire, **Ian Pollock** is generally known by his surname alone. He studied at Manchester College of Art and Design then moved to London to gain a Masters at the Royal College of Art. He spent the next 20 years in London working as an illustrator where he was at the forefront of contemporary illustration and described as "an inspiration to a generation". Pollock worked for all the major newspapers, supplements and magazines on both sides of the Atlantic including The Times, Observer, New Yorker, Penthouse, Playboy and Rolling Stone. In the late 90's Pollock returned to his roots in Cheshire, continuing to work as an illustrator completing posters for RSC productions and a set of stamps for the Royal Mail, book covers for publishers in the UK and Germany and fully illustrated versions of Milton's Paradise Lost for the Folio Society and a cartoon version of King Lear.

Now living and working on the edge of the Peak District he is producing his own work; a series based on the Miracles and Parables of Christ, another on the New Testament and one for the 10 Commandments. In 2001 he was awarded an honorary Doctorate in Arts by Wolverhampton University.

His work has been shown selectively over the years in London and the North of England and has included a retrospective at the National Theatre, South Bank, London.

Wow... Thirty five years since The Association of Illustrators First Annual. I'd have worked for anyone in those days, probably did; I was of mercenary disposition supplying arms to all sides, a freelance sniper with a maladaptive mindset, tip toeing through the minefield of political correctness. My conscience was clear: drawing never hurt anyone. I studied illustration at Manchester Poly and the Royal College of Art, punk was being pretty vacant on the Kings Road, I had no idea what a computer was and the mobile phone was science fiction. I was gloriously naïve... and the AOI was in its infancy calling out to the closet cases with their airbrushes and grant enlargers.

Back then illustration was predominantly black and white, colour was not the default. I learnt my trade in black and white, I still think in black and white. When colour crossed the picket lines I had to learn how to fill-in with my little box of watercolours, and there was no going back. Work ebbed and flowed under the misapprehension of exponential growth. I couldn't have been busier. I was even told I could retire at the age of forty five. What a strange idea. I never went into this business to retire early. Illustration will retire me when it's ready. I grew into illustration because I loved drawing. British illustration flourished, and there was a lot of work around, not just covers but generous inside spreads as well, editorial took off; then the newspapers went coloured. Work was flooding in - and from across "the pond" too as British art directors emigrated and took their favourite illustrators with them: double-page this, double page that, always needed by yesterday. Illustration was thriving. Today it is hard to recall when I last delivered a double-page spread, or

when a courier last lost my artwork on the way to Heathrow, or when an after-draught sucked an A1 illustration from under my arm and chased the departing underground train into the tunnel. Today I scan and hit "send", and live in absolute terror of losing my internet connection.

I have never fully embraced the digital age. I wasn't turned on by it - just another tool with great potential but equally limiting, to say nothing of the unforeseen consequences of not having to chase unreturned artwork with an AOI sticker on the back reminding the industry that "this original remains the property of the artist and must be returned". Less personal contact, less face to face, no sharing hangovers, no blaming the Royal Mail, no going through industrial sized plans-chests in editorial offices hoping to liberate a coveted original on behalf of ... (daren't name names) and holding onto it until they forget. Suffice to say I have originals by Peter Till, Chloe Cheese, Carolyn Gowdy, Robert Mason, Ralph Steadman, Sue Coe, Anne Howeson, Russell Mills, Quentin Blake, Tony Ross, David Hughes and many more, not all legitimately acquired. Those that aren't in frames sit aloft a mountain of my own artwork, and I sometimes wish I could, with a touch of the mouse, reduce the whole lot to the size of a memory stick

After a third of a century I'm back in the closet. Now, more than ever, we need to unite and support the AOI in its efforts to protect the interests of us cabin-fevered, and the closets to come, from the unforeseen consequences of the digital age.

Ian's work is featured on pages 166-167.

2000

2001

2004

2005

2007

2008

2009

2011

JUDGES

The marks awarded by the jury for originality,
artistic ability and fulfilment of the brief
determined which images were given an award or
invited to feature in the book.

Judges
Fred Flade • Sam Freeman • Sheri Gee

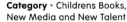

Fred Flade • Design Director, Poke London
Fred is design director at digital creative agency Poke in London.

He has 14 years experience in the industry working across design disciplines with a focus on digital design. Born in Munich, Germany, Fred worked in an advertising agency in Munich before moving to London in 1994 to professionally develop a growing passion for design. He studied at Ravensbourne College of Design and Communication.

Fred co-founded digital communications agency de-construct in 2001, worked as executive creative director with international clients such as Panasonic and Adidas, and won major awards with sites for designer Vince Frost, the Barbican Centre, Panasonic and others.

Category • Childrens Books, New Media and New Talent
"Overall I was hugely impressed by the diversity of work and the fantastic quality of illustration work submitted. It certainly made judging the award a very inspiring experience. I for my part am going to do everything to encourage the use of illustration in more digital and interactive projects."

Sam Freeman • Art Director, Design Week magazine
Sam Freeman is Art Director of Design Week magazine, where he is currently advising on the creation of the Design Week iPad app. Having begun his career in the design studio environment, Freeman moved over to magazines eight years ago, and has overseen the redesigns of publications including Design Week and the Big Issue. He has also worked in the music industry, including a year long stint as art director at James Lavelle's label Surrender. Freeman's design inspirations are Mo Wax creative director Ben Drury and Wired US art director Scott Daddich. His design style is minimal, with a strong focus on typography.

Category • Design and Self Promotion
"A generally excellent standard of work submitted made the judging process a complete joy. A vast array of styles and techniques were evident and picking clear winners certainly wasn't a easy decision to make – and that's credit to all of the illustrators involved."

Sheri Gee • Art Director, The Folio Society
Sheri studied illustration at The Kent Institute of Art and Design Maidstone (now UCA Maidstone), graduating in 1997. Some months later she started at The Folio Society as Production Assistant. Following several changes of role within the company, through Production Controller to Production Manager, Sheri was made Art Director in 2010. 'I count myself very lucky to have worked with some of this country's and increasingly the world's best illustrators. I'm often blown away by the creative response and sheer talent I'm presented with'.

Category • Advertising, Books and Editorial
"I was really honoured to be asked to judge for the AOI, and valued the experience. There was some great work in the mix - instantly recognisable seasoned illustrators, pared with a wealth of work from new talent. The final judging process was hard, narrowing the selection down, weighing up the appropriateness of illustration to brief etc, but I think we got there."

Judges

Martin Harrison • Mike Jolley • James Joyce • Geoffrey Pais • Martin Premm-Jones • Harriet Russell

Martin Harrison • Senior Designer, The Times

Martin Harrison graduated from Norwich School of Art in 1976. He worked as a freelance illustrator before joining The Times in 1993 where, as Design Editor on several Saturday sections, he has promoted greater use of illustration.

He has organised and curated two exhibitions for the acclaimed reportage illustrator, Matthew Cook, designing the catalogues and raising sponsorship: Matthew Cook: The Times War Artist, held at the Coningsby Gallery in 2005, and Sketches from Afghanistan, held at the Ministry of Defence in 2009. Both exhibitions received national media coverage.

Martin has been a judge for AOI Images 28, and a nominator for the Arts Foundation 2008 Illustration Fellowship, where his choice of Swava Harasymowicz won first prize.

Category • Advertising, Books and Editorial

"Working for a newspaper means making fast decisions to tight deadlines. So I appreciated having the time to discuss thoroughly the finalists with the other judges who approached the task with a different perspective from my own. As a result our choices were made with a mix of passion and reason – the way it should be."

Mike Jolley • Art Director, Templar Publishing

Mike has worked at Templar, on and off, since leaving Art School in the 80's. Apart from a brief stint working in a design agency in Amsterdam, he has always worked in children's books.

He currently primarily oversees Templar's picture book list, but has also designed numerous other formats. Mike has also authored several books for children.

He most enjoys creative use of typography and working closely with an amazing roster of illustrators, like Simon Bartram, Helen Ward, Grahame Baker-Smith, and newcomers Levi Pinfold and Owen Davey to name a few. 'I think of myself as more of a stylist and facilitator, than a designer. Helping talented people to realise the book they have in their minds eye', he says.

Category • Children's Books, New Media and New Talent

"I particularly enjoyed the range of entrants in all categories. It is always hard to pitch such diverse styles against one another when it comes to awarding a mark, so at the end of the day the 'Image' itself had to win through, regardless of technique or brief, at least for me."

James Joyce • Graphic Artist and Designer

James Joyce is a London based graphic artist and designer. His work uses bold lines and graphic shapes, and often includes typography and strong colour to produce powerful, ideas-based imagery.

James's distinctive graphic style has attracted commissions from a raft of international clients including Wallpaper*, The New York Times, Nike, Levi's and the BBC and he has been featured in many books and journals including Eye, Creative Review, IdN and Varoom. James has also shown work in various exhibitions including a solo show at Kemistry Gallery, London.

Category • Advertising, Books and Editorial

Geoffrey Pais • Producer, BBC Learning

Geoffrey Pais is a commissioning online producer for BBC Learning. He considers himself very fortunate to be in a position where he can work with talented, creative people - illustrators, comic artists, designers, writers and game developers, as well as fellow colleagues in producing websites aimed at educating and informing Britain's students, parents and teachers.

Geoff has commissioned and produced work for illustrated sites, including BBC Schools Primary History.

Category • Children's Books, New Media and New Talent

"I was very impressed with the high standard of illustration, and encouraged to see accomplished, skilful and imaginative pieces that were clearly the result of a lot of hard work."

Martin Premm-Jones • Director, Premm Design Ltd

Founder of Premm, a branding and design implementation company based in London. Martin enjoys working with a great team of people and is constantly motivated by their never ending creative solutions to client briefs. He has worked with the BBC, BT, Barbican Centre, Barclays, LSO, Clifford Chance and Abercrombie & Kent to name but a few. He says that one of the great aspects of working with such a diverse range of clients from the arts through to corporate organisations is that it gives fantastic opportunities to commission and work with some of the best illustrators around.

Category • Design and Self Promotion

"Judging was a great privilege, but at the same time incredibly difficult. It was great to see the breadth of styles, creativity and originality, you just wish you could commission even more illustration!"

Harriet Russell • Illustrator

Harriet Russell studied illustration at Glasgow School of Art and Central Saint Martins, where she completed her MA in 2001. She has worked for many clients in the UK, US and Europe, mainly within publishing, design and editorial. As well as commissioned work, Harriet has written and illustrated several of her own books, including four children's titles for Italian publisher Edizioni Corraini, whom she collaborates with regularly. Her book of creatively addressed mail 'Envelopes' was published by Allison and Busby in 2008.

She has always enjoyed both drawing and writing, and more often than not her ideas are born of a playful approach with words and images.

Category • Design and Self Promotion

"I found judging Images 35 to be a very enjoyable but difficult process - there were so many entries of a high standard, particularly in the self-promotion category. As an illustrator myself I have a strong sense of what I like - so the thing I found most difficult about the process was to try and put aside personal taste and look objectively for images that had that extra spark of originality or magic - something special about them to make them stand out from the rest."

Critic's Award
Selected by Bonnie Greer

Bonnie Greer is a playwright, author and critic.

She is the librettist for Errolyn Wallen's opera "Yes" for The Royal Opera, Covent Garden. Her latest book is "Langston Hughes: the Value Of Contradiction."

Bonnie has been a critic for BBC2's "NewsNight Review", and her documentary "Reflecting Skin" on the Black image in Western Art was shown on BBC4.

She is a board member of the Serpentine Gallery, and of the British Museum, as well as an artist-in-residence at Somerset House.

Bonnie Greer was awarded the OBE for services to the arts in the Queen's Birthday Honours in 2010.

There were over 400 selected submissions this year, and each communicated not only its remit, but went beyond that to take you to another place. I enjoyed them all.

But it was Peter Strain's "Trying To Poke A Hole In The World" which made articulate that great unspoken that every illustration strives for.

It immediately transmits that "I didn't know that I felt like that" jolt that is a kind of Holy Grail. It is literal and literary, a word portrait whose words are inside of our heads. It invites us to write a script we have never written before.

And yet, it also has a music within that can't be communicated because it is being born and has not yet found its voice. That we all know this music is testament to our connectiveness, which Strain invites us to confront and honour.

There are points where the artist goes back in time to an era in which people did aim to poke a hole in the world, yet he is not nostalgic. Like a twenty first century Rimbaud, he uses this trip down memory land to throw away everything that he reveres. We chase behind, attempting to retrieve what we love, what we know. In the process, we learn something new. Mixed in with the known are those images that are creatures of his imagination, filtered through his

essence. We think that we know them, and their surface familiarity gives us the assurance to step inside the world of the illustration.

There we discover that everything is a product of an apocalyptic imagination. These are drawings about the edge of the abyss. They are a warning to our age, and they're not kidding. The shape of the illustration is like an ancient African gourd. We know that ancient shape in our gut and we respond. I love the throwaway aspect of "Trying To Poke A Hole In The World", too. It is like a piece of graffiti hidden under a railway bridge, or something glimpsed from a car waiting at a traffic light in a "bad" neighbourhood. Its melancholia, its fear, its music and hope and determination does what it says on the tin. Peter Strain reached down deep. He invites you to do the same, too.

Other outstanding work in no particular order: Bill McConkey "Kaleidescope", a cornucopia of what he likes to draw, his visual influences, and stuff from his childhood; Naomi Tipping "GAD", the voyage inside a mental disorder, blunt and clear and beautiful; John Barrett "The King" – this is the deep Latino/Hispanic/Native American/African soul of New York City; Gwen Turner "Dawn in Dalesville;"

"Growth", "Commuters" – 19th Nervous Breakdown in watercolour, pen and ink. You know this world and you're afraid that you live there; Lizzie Mary Cullen "Zizzi Italian Restaurants, Covent Garden" – when the wall mural makes the food taste better, you have a winner; Christiane Engel "Locals Only - London" – this is the real city that never sleeps; Becky Brown "Travelling Circus" – everyone's archetypal old box in the corner that yields unexpected treasure; Michael Hutchinson "We Can't Rewind" – you don't have to understand English to get the message of this illustration. The truth, pure and simple; Liam Derbyshire "GTC Spying" – Big Brother alive and well and in your own workplace. Chilling and direct.

Peter Strain
Trying To Poke A Hole In The World

Category Self Promotion
Medium Pen and ink, coloured digitally
Brief Create an image that depicts people from various walks of life struggling to make their mark.

Peter Strain is a designer/illustrator from Northern Ireland, currently enjoying a residency at the University of Ulster, School of Art and Design, Belfast, from which he graduated in 2010 with a degree in Visual Communication.
Specialising in creating carefully composed hand rendered illustration and typography using a fairly limited colour palette, he's a firm believer that less is more.
Whilst tackling social, political and cultural issues with bold imagery and dark/bittersweet humour, Peter tries to sprinkle elements of his own personal fixations from the worlds of comics, music, lyric and film into his work.

Visit peterstrain.co.uk for more of his work.

Advertising • Essay
Jim Davies • Founder of copywriting studio totalcontent

Jim Davies is a commercial writer and cultural commentator.

He's helped clients like Paul Smith, Orange, Royal Mail and Nokia with everything from naming and one-liners to ads, books, web sites and annual reports.

His articles have appeared in specialist design and advertising titles including Eye, Print, Campaign and Design Week as well as the Guardian, Daily Telegraph, Financial Times and Sunday Times Magazine.

In 2008, he was awarded the creative industry's top award – a D&AD Gold – for his contribution to the National Gallery's 'Grand Tour', conceived by the Partners. He has sat on creative juries for D&AD, BAFTA and Design Week.

Everywhere you look, belts are being tightened and budgets are being slashed. Like the rest of us, the advertising industry is having to take stock and reinvent itself for this new era of austerity. Adland's erstwhile reputation for wanton extravagance is gradually starting to ebb, as agencies not only try to find ways to make clients' money go further, but also to stay in step with the times – chiming, reflecting and taking inspiration from what's happening out there on the streets.

Which, paradoxically, is good news for illustrators. Lavish photographic productions and epic commercials are not only unaffordable, but also ill-advised, as they sit uncomfortably with audiences whose current reality is so far removed from them. Ideas, of course, are still the prime currency of advertising, but nowadays creatives are having to think differently and carefully about the media in which they are executed, and how best to present the flowers of their imagination.

And illustration is proving just the job. No concept is too surreal or ambitious – the illustrator just needs to play it all out in their mind's eye and have the skill to reproduce it. Virtually any style is possible – from the faux naïf doodlings of David Shrigley or Tom Gauld to the slick hyper-realism of Nick Ainley or a 3Di. For any switched-on art director, this almost infinite choice of visual talent is like being a small child

in a sweetshop, not knowing which sticky delight to grab hold of next.

It's not just about surface styling either. In a distrusting, questioning world, there's also a certain disarming sincerity about illustration that can cut through the cynicism. Rough edges, pencil slips, wonky perspectives, work that's deliberately under-finessed or unfinished, lends contemporary illustration its peculiar charm. To the audience, there's something reassuringly authentic about the hand-made aesthetic of illustration – it's visceral and direct, human mark-making that seems to reach out of the page and touch us.

While illustrated characters have been a mainstay of advertising for decades – just think of John Gilroy's menagerie for Guinness, Will Owen's Bisto Kids, or more recently, Mandeville & Wenlock, the blingy 3D mascots of the 2012 London Olympics created by Iris – lately, the illustrated canvas seems to have broadened.

Now we're tending to see more self-contained illustrated worlds, like Andy Smith's poster for the British Heart Foundation, which shows hundreds of line-drawn characters exercising in a 'Where's Wally?'-like tableaux. The detail is breathtaking, yet the bright yellow background and the huge structural 60 in the middle (denoting the 60-minutes of exertion we're supposed to take each day), help retain its power as a poster.

Elsewhere, Katherin Baxter creates exquisite 3D topographic landscapes, which the Times head of design David Driver describes as like being "transported by hot air balloon, floating gently over all those much loved and beautifully painted landscapes". Curiously devoid of people, her meticulous axonometric projections have been used as promotional posters for the Times and London Syon Park Hotel in Brentford, as well as a huge eight-metre foyer mural at the Runnymede Thames Hotel.

Anglo-German illustrator Serge Seidlitz goes one step further by creating the buzzing, densely populated 'Island of Swizerland' for the Euro soft drink brand Sinalco. While the Barcelona-based brothers Brosmind have actually taken on the whole world in a campaign for Land Rover that show how the car helps you escape from your super-stressful everyday life, to find peace and quiet on the opposite side of the globe.

Playful and witty, these conceptual illustrations are all about giving a promising idea physical form, adding another dimension through charm and character. Because they have their own reality, normal rules don't apply, and the improbable, even the physically impossible, are readily embraced by the audience.

Though there's still a bit of it around, these illustrated worlds represent a

Clockwise from top:
Kleenex by Gail Armstrong
60 Minutes by Andy Smith
Hyundai by Peter Grundy
Sinalco by Serge Seidlitz
Endsleigh ad by Ciara Phelan
Land Rover ad by Brosmind
Marmite by Al Murphy for DDB
London Syon Park Hotel by Katherine Baxter

natural progression from the recently popular media mash-up where a personality or central character is photographed and then placed in front of a swirling, patterned illustrated background. We've seen this recently in Airside's vibrant graphics and programme banners for the Asian network website, animated form for the titles for Jamie Oliver's Channel 4 series Dream School by Passion Pictures, and Ruth Rowland's posters touting the tourist delights of Aruba.

Long-time student insurers Endsleigh also used the technique in press ads featuring illustration by Ciara Phelan, where she visualises a typical student's personal belongings from 45 years ago (lava lamps and vinyl records) in contrast to today (laptops and iPods). Part of an ongoing campaign, each time an illustrator's work appears, they are clearly credited and the name of their college also appears to highlight the company's strong ties with the NUS.

Even ideas which are polar opposites can be conveyed in the same ad through illustration. Like Gail Armstrong's series of intricate paper sculptures for a JWT-commissioned Kleenex campaign. These work right-way up or upside-down to show paired, contrasting worlds of success and failure, colour and drabness, heaven and hell. Armstrong seamlessly combines sophisticated storytelling with an elegant, slightly

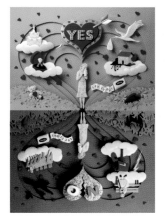

knowing, humour, demonstrating that you need tissues whether you're crying tears of joy or sorrow.

A couple of years ago, Marmite (through the agency DDB) used a similar device with bold, simple flat-colour images by Al Murphy incorporating a deceptively clever trompe l'oeil effect. Look at them one way, and they illustrate love of the divisive brown spread. Skew them sideways or upside down and that love turns to hate. So we see a hand putting a Marmite rice cake into an eager open mouth. But flip the page, and it becomes a hand flushing the cake down the toilet pan.

Once again, illustration proves it can provide the instant hit that advertising messages need to cut through. Far less memory hungry than photography, it is proving its worth in digital media, as well as its traditional printed media home. What's more, the rise of illustrated infographics, epitomised by David McCandless' 'Information is Beautiful' book, has shown that illustration can be used to convey complex ideas and narrative in advertising as well as editorial – like Peter Grundy's typically engaging posters for Hyundai, which elegantly outline the car maker's eco credentials.

Advertising began life with illustration as its closest ally and the relationship is still going strong. It may be tough out there, but at least illustration is enjoying a rich vein of form.

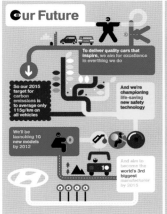

Advertising • Gold Award

Rose Lloyd
Spring Family Concert

Medium Digital and mixed media
Brief A classical orchestral concert with a Spring theme. Aimed at children and their parents. The concert is very 'family' orientated and is much more relaxed than our normal format.
Commissioned by David Sedgwick
Client 999 Design
Commissioned for BBC Philharmonic

Rose Lloyd is a Manchester based illustrator who returned to full time education, graduating from Stockport College in 2009 with a BA Hons in Visual Art & Design, specialising in illustration. She has a studio in an old cotton mill where she experiments with texture and print techniques. Over the last two years her style has been developing into one she hopes will be recognisable with her combination of texture, shape, bold use of colour and a suggestion of humour. Her work has appeared in a cross section of magazines such as Design Week, Your M&S, Landscape Magazine, Nursing Standard, Times Educational Supplement and Radio Times.

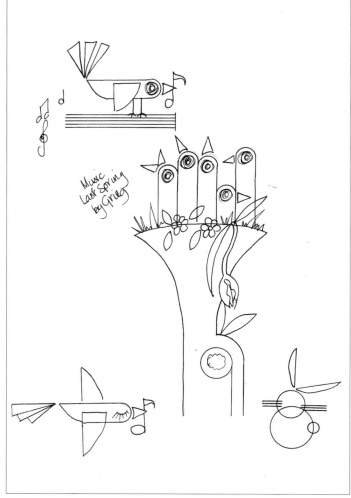

Serge Seidlitz
Seawolf Class Attack

Medium Pen and ink
Brief Draw a densely populated Jungle scene, with a giant submarine in the middle that you can't miss. Tagline 'Find the Seawolf-class attack to win free checking'.
Commissioned by Danielle Borden
Client TDAAD
Commissioned for First Bank

An English/German hybrid, born in Kenya in 1977, **Serge Seidlitz** grew up traveling between the UK and Asia, where a diet of MTV and Mad magazine fueled his desire to become an illustrator. Serge combines elements of popular culture with these diverse influences to create a body of work which both relates back to an iconic graphic language and also explores innovative and original ideas through maps, information graphics, character design and much more.

After studying Graphic Design at Camberwell College of Art he worked as a designer in-house at The Cartoon Network before leaving to concentrate on illustration - he has an ever evolving list of clients including MTV, AOL, Virgin, Estrella, Channel Four, ITV, Barclays, Vh1, Volvic, Orange, JWT, John Brown, The Times, BBH, BBDO, Leo Burnett, Sinalco, BBC, RKCR/Y&R, First Bank, Hicklin Slade, Honda, Vodafone, Baileys, British Airways, Red bull, Wired, Dorling Kindersly, Raiffheisen, Simon & Shuster, Elisava School of Design, Macmillan, The Guardian, GQ, and NME magazine. Serge is represented in London by Debut Art. His website and blog are updated regularly with new work at sergeseidlitz.com and sergeseidlitz.tumblr.com.

Advertising • Bronze Award

Frances Castle
Bear Hug

Medium Digital
Brief To produce an appealing image to promote
Frances' work and also Arena Illustration. This
image should then be adapted for use on an
online banner advertisement.
Commissioned by Caroline Thomson
Client Arena Illustration

Frances Castle studied Illustration at
Lincoln College of Art, then Computer
Imaging and animation at London
Guildhall University. She worked in
the computer games industry for over
10 years, creating in-game graphics
and animations for Play Station
games. In 2003 she decided to give
up steady employment, and after a
short period developing her portfolio
she went freelance. Since then she has
worked on a wide range of projects
from magazine illustration, to pop-up
books and interactive websites. This is
Frances' second award from the AOI.
Last year she won bronze in the New
Media category.

Books • Essay
Sheri Gee • Art Director, The Folio Society

Sheri studied illustration at The Kent Institute of Art and Design Maidstone (now UCA Maidstone), graduating in 1997. Some months later she started at The Folio Society as Production Assistant. Following several changes of role within the company, through Production Controller to Production Manager, Sheri was made Art Director in 2010. 'I count myself very lucky to have worked with some of this country's and increasingly the world's best illustrators. I'm often blown away by the creative response and sheer talent I'm presented with'.

It may be a cliché but it's true that we're apt to judge a book by its cover. Authors should be thankful, then, for the continual progression of great cover design and likewise of designers around at the moment. You'll see them celebrated on Fwis' covers site[1], or The Book Cover Archive[2], to name a few of the online resources. Illustration has long been the mainstay of some of the best book covers. Take a look at, for example, the fantastic selection of traditional bindings on the Beauty for Commerce site, run by The University of Rochester[3], USA. And I'm glad to say illustration continues to be at the forefront of great book cover design today.

But in my job as Art Director at The Folio Society, I'm called to go beyond cover art alone, commissioning interior art, for our illustrated editions of the classics and modern classics. We're not so much re-illustrating the classics, as many of the books we publish have never been available in an illustrated format before, so it's a totally fresh challenge. Sometimes the approach is to commission illustration true to period, as if we were publishing the first edition, sometimes we're looking to bring a fresh take on a

novel. What we hope to achieve is an excellent marriage of text and image, complementing the narrative with, in general, a series of six to twelve full-page colour or black and white plates. The company has been a proud supporter of illustration, commissioning some of the best illustrators this country, and increasingly the world, has produced since 1947.

Being one of the few British publishers to go beyond the cover makes it all the harder to find appropriate illustrators. Unless someone is doing a personal or college project with us in mind, I'm often unlikely to find sequential narrative fiction illustration in the every day portfolio, and if there is, it is more likely to be in the range of children's rather than adult books. That's not to say I'm not frequently presented with great work, but it's often that bit harder to envisage how someone used to dealing with editorial or advertising clients will tackle a story, repetition of characters, historic detail etc.

One such challenge has been with Folio's series of Andrew Lang Rainbow Fairy Books. Published from 1889, Lang brought out a series of books,

collections of world folk tale and lore, running to twelve volumes, from The Blue Fairy Book through to Lilac. The collection has stories from many of the greats, the Brothers Grimm, Perrault, Hans Christian Andersen – housing such famous stories as 'Little Red Riding Hood', 'Puss in Boots' and 'Hansel and Gretel'. Folio has been publishing the series since 2003, bringing out one or two volumes a year, looking to publish the last in the collection in 2013.

The aim has always been to commission illustration true to the period, to retain a certain Rackham charm, but to ensure each edition uses a different illustrator. As the illustration medium becomes increasing digital, it's been no easy task, but I'm glad to say I've worked with some extremely talented illustrators and we've had some amazing results.

Anyone who takes on a commission for this series has quite a deal to do – each book comprises a line-drawn endpaper and title page, together with on average eleven line illustrations to be integrated with the text and thirteen full page colour plates, not forgetting the binding design, which is full bound in cloth, traditionally blocked

Clockwise from top: Group shot of Folio Society's Fairy Books
Illustration by Robert Venables from The Violet Fairy Book
Illustration by Omar Rayyan from The Brown Fairy Book
Illustration by Niroot Puttapipat from The Red Fairy Book
Cover by Anna & Elena Balbusso from Northanger Abbey, Study Guide, published by Black Cat Publishing
Illustration by Iassen Ghiuselev for Queen of Spades, published by The Grimm Press

in four colours. The first volume, The Blue Fairy Book, was illustrated by Canadian artist Charles van Sandwyk, who produced a charming collection for us. Each artist since has had rather large boots to fill, and a beautiful style to sustain. Throughout the series so far we've had the pleasure of working with Debra McFarlane (The Pink Fairy Book), Danuta Mayer (The Yellow Fairy Book), Julian de Narvaez (The Green Fairy Book), Bob Venables (The Violet Fairy Book), Omar Rayyan (The Brown Fairy Book), and Niroot Puttapipat (The Red Fairy Book). Niroot won Bronze in Images 34, Book category, for his Folio illustrations for Russian Myths and Legends. I'm currently working with two more artists on the next two Fairy books – Crimson and Grey, with three more titles to go... and a few illustrators up my sleeve!

Having seen a wealth of amazing illustration in my career, it's evident that the illustrated adult fiction title is alive and well, not only here, but internationally. Just take a look at the portfolio from Anna and Elena Balbusso to see evidence of this. Though much of the work of these two Italian illustrators may have been commissioned for the young adult or even student reader, the titles have certainly enlivened the classic genre. For example, their wonderful and award-winning illustrations for Charlotte Brontë's Jane Eyre and Northanger Abbey, for Black Cat Publishing's study guides; a series for Le Horla by Guy De Maupassant or Tristan et Iseult for Éditions Milan. Or look at Iassen Ghiuselev, a Bulgarian illustrator who has produced some stunningly detailed work for titles such as Pushkin's The Queen of Spades, Don Quixote, Oliver Twist, etc, for a myriad of international publishers from Germany to Taiwan.

With the birth of the Kindle and other such devices, I see no reason why illustrated adult fiction shouldn't continue to thrive, which should be a great excitement for many illustrators. Thankfully for me, The Folio Society continues to embrace great illustration, which keeps me on the search for outstanding work for our illustrated editions in traditional book form.

Footnotes
1 covers.fwis.com
2 bookcoverarchive.com
3 lib.rochester.edu/index.cfm?page=3352

Caroline List
Helianthus

Medium Collage
Brief Illustrate a set of poems by the writer
Jane McKie.
Commissioned by Jane McKie
Client Knucker Press

Since graduating with an MDes from
Edinburgh College of Art in 2008,
Caroline List has made her first
forays into the often difficult world of
children's book publishing and has
taken part in exhibitions in Britain,
Cyprus, the US and Canada. She has
also worked with a range of small local
publishers who have supported her
love of experimenting with collage,
geometrical forms, bold colours and
the white space of book pages.

Mostly she can be found in her tiny
studio in the heart of Edinburgh, where
she busily works on turning carelessly
abandoned bits and pieces into
something visually exciting.

Jonathan Burton
A Bowl Of Petunias And A Surprised
Looking Whale

Medium Pencil and digital
Brief 'They would appear,' said Ford doubtfully,
'to have turned into a bowl of petunias and a
very surprised looking whale.' A scene from the
book The Hitchhikers Guide to the Galaxy by
Douglas Adams.
Commissioned by Gavin Morris
Client The Folio Society

Jonathan Burton has worked as an
illustrator since 1999 after graduating
with a MA from Kingston University,
London. His work has appeared on
covers and in the pages of TIME,
Nature, New Scientist, The Times
and many more magazines and
newspapers. Additional clients of note
include The Folio Society, Penguin
Books, and The BBC. There have been
other awards from the Association of
Illustrators for Editorial, Advertising
and Book illustration as well as a Silver
medal from the Society of Illustration in
New York. He now lives with his family
in Bordeaux, France.

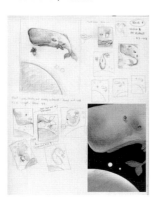

Books • Bronze Award

Rod Hunt
Paddy Clarke Ha Ha Ha

Medium Digital
Brief Illustrate the the cover of Roddy Doyle's
Booker Prize winning book.
Commissioned by Michael Salu
Client Random House

Rod Hunt is a London based
Illustrator who has built a reputation
for retro tinged Illustrations and
detailed character filled landscapes
for UK and international clients
spanning publishing, design,
advertising and new media, for
everything from book covers to
advertising campaigns, theme park
maps and even the odd large scale
installation too!

Rod is also the artist behind the
bestselling books 'Where's Stig?' and
'Where's Stig? The World Tour' for the
BBC's hit TV show Top Gear.

Des McCannon is an illustrator, designer, writer and academic. She has illustrated children's books for Bloomsbury and worked as a character designer in Tokyo, and now lives near Liverpool with her husband and two children. She teaches on the BA and MA illustration courses at Glyndwr and also lectures on the history and theory of visual literacy. Her interests lie in decorative art and folk art origins of contemporary illustration. She has run research projects that investigate the use of illustration in primary school curriculum, looking at how children draw conceptual ideas by creating allegorical narratives. "Illustration is of enormous, often overlooked, cultural value as it is through illustration that collective memories of places and times can be stored, childhood books being a powerful example".

Creating a memorable and successful children's picture book is something many of my students aspire to achieve. It is possible to teach the basics of character development, composition and visual narrative flow, and a student's personal visual language will develop through extensive experimentation with drawing and media. However, often whether their picture book story 'works' depends upon the emotional core of the book. The 'heart' of a book, and its appeal to a young audience is not necessarily always about the story, important though the narrative is. Books offer a total experience, for a child – from the excitement of choosing one from a shelf of options, to the strong bond created with others through sharing, looking and listening, and the enjoyment derived from the many tactile qualities the book affords. These experiences are not mediated through the eyes and ears alone, but involve a huge number of sensory, emotional and cognitive factors for both the child and the adult involved in the book.

If you think back to the books you loved as a child, they might not all have been conventional picture books. I remember once hearing Nick Sharratt give a talk about what had inspired him to become an illustrator, and he showed us a 1950's cookery book with hidden illustrations and split pages, which had mesmerized him as a child.

With the current industry trend towards adapting picture book formats for digital media it is worth reflecting on the tactile qualities that only a book can deliver. The feel of the paper, the way the ink lies on the page, the smell of ink and paper and glue, the comforting bulk of a favourite book hugged against your chest, to be stashed under a pillow after being read for the hundredth time. Soft dog eared pages, mildew on the end papers of old books, pop ups, tabs to pull (and eventually destroy), the potential in a book for you to colour in all your favourite characters orange (something I did as a child, though I am not sure why I thought this improved them). Picture books are tactile and involve many aspects of a child's sensory intelligence as well as visual and cognitive logic.

They provide the nexus for a nurturing triangle to occur - when an adult puts their arm around a child to turn the pages. But equally they enable a child to be alone, in private, intense concentration. A colleague describes her granddaughter sitting on the bedroom floor for hours with a pile of books to one side and the regular 'thunk', of a book finished with, ready for the next one, coming from her room.

The level of engagement with a book by a child is more than just the story and the pictures. I have been constantly surprised by my children's

taste in books. They love the dog eared softbacks of my own childhood; 'Meal One' by Ivor Cutler and Helen Oxenbury, 'In the Night Kitchen' by Maurice Sendak - books that look muted and melancholy in the brightly coloured cheerful panoply of many books on offer to children today. These books have arrived into my children's lives pre-loved, pre-scribbled upon, palimpsests suggesting other childhoods, other readers, their aura of personal history is perhaps part of their charm.

Books live in the mind, and children love to draw their favourite characters, extend the narrative, imagine other possibilities for the world of the book. They love to play make believe, and 'be' the character too. A good picture book character holds the potential for many stories. The child can identify with, almost become the character. This helps build empathy and the make believe experimenting with identities offers the child myriad ways of becoming themselves. Stereotyping of gender roles and abilities in children's books channels this experimentation, creating self consciousness about play where there ought to be none.

How will digital publishing impact on how stories are told? It is magical to draw your finger across a screen and see things move – Oliver Jeffers' 'The Heart and the Bottle' is a good example. However, the

distinction between a good story and a game needs to be made. A story is something that you are told, it has form and the images are significant, almost symbolic. 'Interactive' stories, by offering the potential for many possible twists and endings do not challenge the reader to follow the internal logic of the story, to see correspondences and symmetries in the plot in the same way. A good story is not about choice, it is about reaching an understanding about a problem or dilemma.

With both Puffin Books and Bologna now offering prizes for the development of digital books, this is obviously a growth area for work for illustrators (let us resist the label content providers, as long as possible) and cannot be ignored. Working collaboratively with animators and computer coders is the practical way to achieve animated and interactive content, unless you are confident about keeping up with the latest developments in technology. It is up to you to decide where your strengths are and where your energy should be focused. More and more illustrators are working in loose collectives, pooling skills and ideas on larger projects. This raises interesting questions about authorship in a world that has been traditionally dominated by big names.

Will digital formats replace the book? Let's hope not. A book doesn't need recharging after a few hours, nor does

it need an expensive (and breakable) interface in order to work. Books have survived changes in technology over the last hundred years. They remain central to the emotional and cognitive development of children. First cinema, then television and now computers have competed for children's attention, and yet the book resists obsolescence. However exciting the potential for digital storytelling is, I believe that books remain a sustainable and democratic medium for children's storytelling to occur in the future.

Heart in the Bottle for iPad by Oliver Jeffers, published by HarperCollins Publishers Ltd, developed by Bold Creative

Cover and inside spread of In The Night Kitchen by Maurice Sendak, published by Red Fox

Cover and inside spread of Meal One by Ivor Cutler and Helen Oxenbury, published by Piccolo Picture Books

Miriam Latimer
The Sunflower Sword

Medium Acrylic
Brief To illustrate the children's book: 'The Sunflower Sword' by Mark Sperring, about a boy who conquers war and hate with the use of a sunflower.
Commissioned by Rona Selby
Client Anderson Press

Miriam Latimer lives and works in a house on a hill in North Devon where she can see the sea.

She graduated in 2003 with a BA Hons in Illustration from Bristol U.W.E. Since then, she has been a freelance Illustrator, mostly concentrating on Children's Book illustration, but she dabbles in a bit of editorial and a bit of writing too. She has illustrated books for Hodder, Barefoot Books, Anderson Press, Kingfisher, Ladybird, A&C Black and Wayland. She works mostly in acrylic, but sometimes you can spot a bit of collage or pencil in there too. She carries her sketchbook everywhere with her, sneakily drawing people whenever she can. In cafés, trains, planes and on the beach, and in the bottom of her bag you will normally find a large assortment of pencils and pens.

If you do not find her painting at her desk, you will find her gazing out of her window, day dreaming of a sunnier climate.

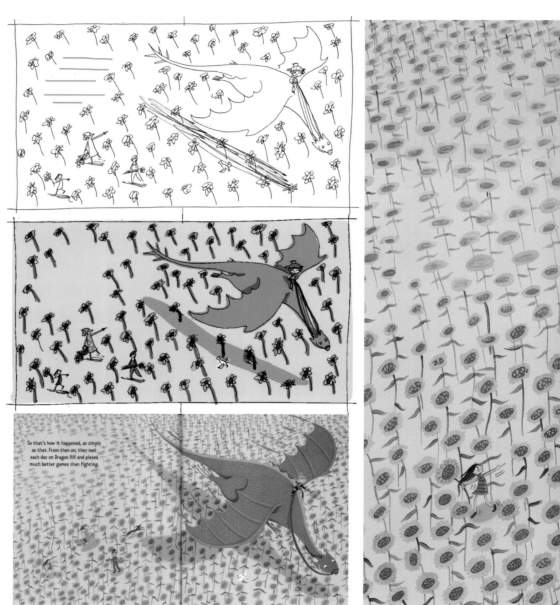

So that's how it happened, as simply as that. From then on, they met each day on Dragon Hill and played much better games than fighting.

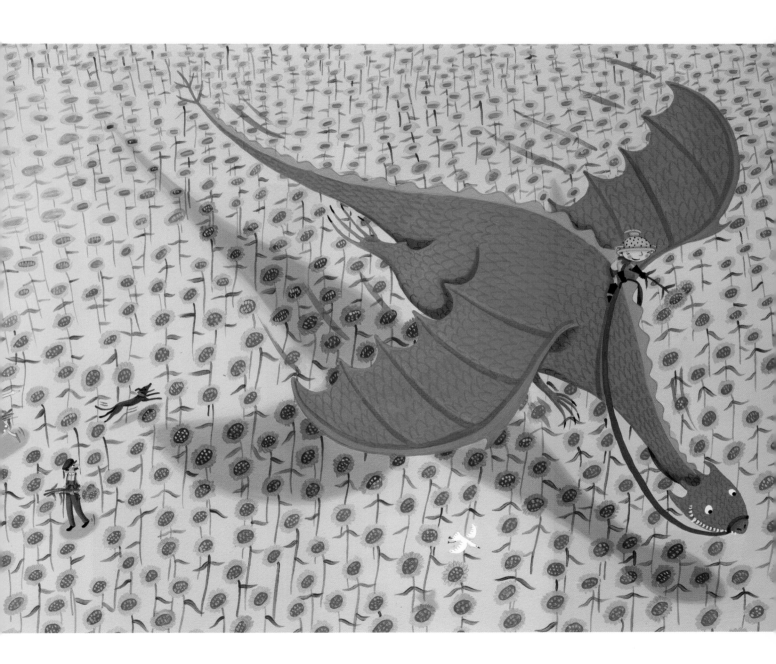

Jason Chapman
One Kiss, One Hug

Medium Digital and mixed media
Brief Opening spread of 'One Kiss, One Hug', one of two story ideas contracted to be published by Random House.
Commissioned by Sue Buswell
Client Random House

Jason Chapman studied at Bradford and Camberwell Colleges of Art. As well as being Battersea Dogs and Cats Home's official illustrator, Jason's illustrations are in permanent exhibitions at the Natural History Museum, Singapore Science Centre, Chicago Field Museum and Living Coasts, Devon. He works regularly with NSPCC on their successful 'Letters From Santa' Campaign.

Jasons debut picture book, 'Ted, Bo and Diz; The first Adventure' was shortlisted for the Best Emerging Illustrator Award at the 2007 Booktrust Early Years Awards. 2009 saw seven books published by Simon & Schuster, Campbell Books and Naxos Books. 'Five Little Ducks' was shortlisted at the 2009 Booktrust Early Years Awards.

'Stan and Mabel' was published by Templar Publishing in 2010 and a second book follows in 2011.

Jason's characters have been animated, often by himself, for educational DVDs and promotional/web use. As well as working on new picture books for leading Publishers, Jason has recently been developing a new children's television programme with Ragcoll Productions.

'One Kiss, One Hug' is published in 2011 by Random House Children's Books with a second title to follow later in the year.

Jason was born in Cambridge, grew up in Bradford and now lives in East Devon with his wife, eight year old son and two younger daughters and works at his studio a few miles away in Dorset.

'. . . and they all lived happily ever after,' whispered Daddy Bear. He kissed and hugged Ben and Ursula goodnight. Ursula went to sleep straight away.

Children's Books • Bronze Award

Garry Parsons
Movie Maker

Medium Digital and mixed media
Brief Everything you need to know to create films
with your digital camera or phone. For children
aged 8+. Illustrations throughout. These images
are for lighting your horror film!
Commissioned by Quarto Children's Books
Client Candlewick Press

Garry Parsons studied Fine Art at
The Kent Institute of Art and Design
followed by the Sequential Design &
Illustration MA at Brighton University.
His editorial illustrations appear
regularly in the UK and USA and his
illustrations have adorned the recently
refurbished 'Pet Kingdom' at Harrods,
book jackets, theatre posters and pet
food packaging.

His illustration for children's books
have won awards and critical acclaim,
working with Kes Gray for Random
House, Jeanne Willis for Puffin, as
well as Julia Donaldson and Malachy
Doyle. Garry has also author illustrated
Krong! Perth & Kinross Word's Out!
Picture Book Prize winner 2006.

Garry recently teamed up with
noted physicist Stephen Hawking and
his daughter Lucy on two fact based
space adventures, George's Secret Key
to the Universe and it's sequel.

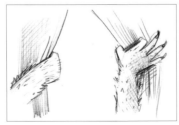

Design • Essay
Adrian Shaughnessy • Graphic Designer and Writer

Adrian Shaughnessy is a graphic designer and writer. In 1989 he co-founded the design company Intro. Today he runs ShaughnessyWorks, a consultancy combining design and editorial direction. He is a founding partner in Unit Editions, a publishing company producing books on design and visual culture. Shaughnessy has written and art directed numerous books on design. From 2006 until 2009, he was editor of Varoom. He has been interviewed frequently on television and radio and lectures extensively around the world. In 2010 he was appointed visiting professor at the Royal College of Art, London. He hosts a radio show called Graphic Design on the Radio on Resonance FM.

The idea that there is an unbridgeable divide between graphic design and illustration is a recent phenomenon. Mostly, designers and illustrators are doing the same thing – communicating a message, telling a story, or conveying information. The only difference is that graphic designers tend to do it with language, and illustrators with imagery.

Yet even that distinction doesn't stand up to scrutiny – the meaning and intention of words is often "illustrated" by designers through their choice of typefaces and the way they position text and words; and illustrators often use decorative or hand rendered lettering in their work. Perhaps what seems like an unbridgeable divide is really a small crack in the ice rather than a gaping ravine?

If we look back through history we see that graphic design and illustration skills have often been found in a single individual. The great Paul Rand moved effortlessly between pure typography and minimalist, art-inspired illustration; Alan Fletcher was both a master of the expressive squiggle and hand drawn logo, and a graphic designer of consummate skill. Milton Glaser might be the finest example of all –a credible graphic designer and an inspirational illustrator and image-maker.

Up until the 1980s it was possible to find individuals who did both

illustration and graphic design. Today, however, it's a rarity to have anyone say I'm a designer and illustrator. Well, OK, let's rephrase that: lots of people say it, but not many do it with the credibility of the trio of masters mentioned above.

This is hardly surprising. Our education system with its separate illustration and graphic design courses dictates that we must be one or the other. But it is my contention that there are convincing and credible graphic designer/illustrators – it's just that the methodologies and definitions have changed.

To test the validity of my view, we have to go back to the 1980s. Prior to the "designer decade", illustrators had been the top dogs. They commanded huge fees and won all the awards and trophies. Illustration was routinely used to spearhead major ad campaigns; it was deployed on everything from blockbuster Hollywood movie posters to the literature issued by high street banks; it was used on record covers, book jackets and posters.

But towards the end of the go-go 1980s, something changed. Graphic designers, not illustrators, became the dominant force in commercial messaging. And if the defining graphic designer of the 1980s was Neville Brody it's worth noting that he was an infrequent user of illustration (though

it would be incorrect to say he never used illustration.) Brody captured the zeitgeist of 80s' hedonism and style obsession through his bold foregrounding of typography and his deft handling of photographic imagery; his page layouts for the Face were the defining templates of the 80s "look" – and it was his typography that made them different.

Not long after Brody's graphic vision exploded over the pages of The Face, graphic designers discovered the power of the computer. This changed everything. Where once designers might have produced their own illustrations – or more likely, commissioned illustrators to create work for them – they now called upon the algorithmic power of the Apple Mac to manipulate images – and lettering – in any way they pleased. The outcome of this was that narrative illustration fell out of fashion and was replaced by an abstract swirl of dots, geometric shapes and – most tellingly – decorative and expressive typography.

Graphic designers now had the tools and know-how to create non-typographic imagery that once would have required the skill and training of an illustrator. Suddenly, designers could reclaim the role they had previously abdicated – the role of the designer/illustrator.

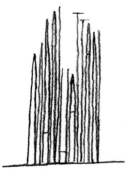

view driving in from the Triboro bridge

I ♥ NY

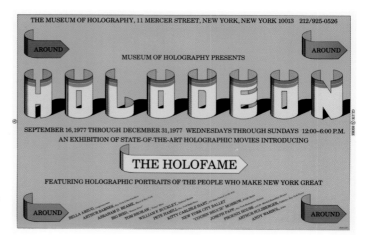

These practitioners only ever call themselves graphic designers, but in truth they are just as much illustrators as designers. I'm thinking of people like Michael Place at Build and Kim Hiorthoy, and studios such as Hort, in Germany. They may not use pens and crayons, they may not use illustration in the traditional story-telling sense, but their reliance on the emotive power of pure shape and pure colour cannot be mistaken for anything other than the authorial impulse of the illustrator to create emotional and atmospheric impact.

Graphic designers – digital natives – who use the computer to extend their range of expression no longer exclusively inhabit a world of non-linguistic communication. It's true that designers have lost the habit of commissioning illustrators – instead they adopt a DIY approach and create the imagery they need using a variety of techniques and software. We can look at this as bad news for traditional illustrators looking for opportunities to practice their craft, or we can look at it as the inevitable evolution of a craft that has once inseparable from graphic design and which has always been at the mercy of technological change.

One thing's for sure: the chasm between designers and illustrators suddenly doesn't look so wide.

Left page:
Alan Fletcher
Manhattan, 1992
Beware Wet Paint, Phaidon Press, 1996
Milton Glaser
I Heart NY, 1977
Holodeon, designed, 1977

Right page:
Build
Objectified logo
Like.No.Other film still
Kim Hiorthoy
Diskjokke: Discolated, record sleeve for Smalltown Supersound, 2010.
Mats Gustafsson and Yoshimi: Words On The Floor, record sleeve for Smalltown Superjazzz, 2007.
Ann and Paul Rand
Cover and inside spread for Sparkle and Spin, 1957, published by Chronicle Books.
Hort
Poster to announce a lecture series during their guest professorship at HFG Offenbach, 2005.
Album inside spread for Booka Shade - The sun and the neon light, 2008, Get Physical Music.

Simon Pemberton
After Dark

Medium Mixed media
Brief Create a unique and distinct mood for Taylors After Dark coffee within its range - a smooth, rich, dark blend visualised as giving a sense of comfort on dark evenings in your home.
Commissioned by Jo Andrade
Client Taylors of Harrogate

Simon Pemberton was born near Liverpool and moved to London to study his MA Illustration at Central St Martins. He now lives and works in London's East End with a studio overlooking London Fields. His illustration work has been commissioned by a wide range of major design, publishing and advertising agencies worldwide. Projects are as diverse as brand development, packaging, book covers, editorial and corporate literature. Clients include Adobe U.K, Fuji, Taylors of Harrogate, The Folio Society, Royal Opera House, Leith Harbour Development, CDT, Lowe, New York Times, L.A Times, Boston Globe, Guardian, Observer, Independent, Blueprint, Financial Times, New Scientist, Tatler, Harper Collins, Penguin, Hodder, Random House Publishing, Readers Digest, BBC Worldwide, etc. Simon is a previous winner of a Books Gold Award, three Silver awards for Books, Editorial and Design and two Bronze awards in the Design and Advertising sections.

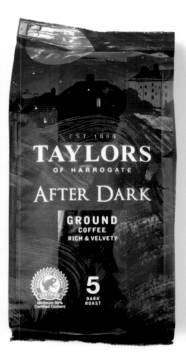

Design • Silver Award

Andy Smith
The Lonely Polygamist

Medium Digital
Brief Create a book jacket for The Lonely Polygamist that illustrates a passage from the novel which refers to a 'large wooden house lit up like a fairground ride'.
Commissioned by Suzanne Dean
Client Random House

Andy Smith studied illustration at the University of Brighton and the Royal College of Art. His work combines illustration and typography to create images that have humour, energy and optimism, executed with a handmade, hand-printed, tactile feel. Quirky characters find themselves in absurd situations, often with a large piece of lettering nearby.

When not producing commercial work for clients such as Nike, Sony, McDonalds, Orange and Mercedes, Andy can be found in his studio by the sea in Hastings screen printing books and posters about Fatty, the Target People and the Hot Dog.

Design • Bronze Award

Charles Williams
Madness

Medium Digital
Brief The AOI commissioned a cover for their
Advertising Directory. It was an open brief, as
long as it referenced advertising in some way…
this is what I did.
Commissioned by Paul Ryding
Client The AOI

Charles Williams is an award-
winning illustrator. He has produced
type and illustration for Nike,
Volkswagen, Adobe and the AOI, and
has recently had work featured in
several exhibitions and publications.
From a graphic design background,
Charles uses a geometric approach to
illustration that utilises depth, texture
and colour to create complex pieces.
He lives in London.

Editorial • Essay
Penny Garrett • Art Director, The Economist

Penny Garrett manages the graphics department of The Economist newspaper and has done so since 1988. The department is responsible for the design and layout of the print and electronic versions of the magazine, including the front cover. She oversaw the redesign of The Economist, which was launched in full colour for the first time in May 2001. She has also worked for the BBC as Art Director of The Listener magazine and for the Daily Telegraph. Penny obtained a BA (Hons) in Editorial and Information Design at Hornsey College of Art (a very long time ago!)

Keeping abreast of "technological advances" is like herding cats. Just when you think you've got one in the bag, another one dashes out. You've no idea where it came from, or what to do with it and anyway it's moving so fast you won't stand a chance of catching it.

Welcome to my world.
Like most sane people, I'm not a huge fan of technology for its own sake. I confess I am a traditionalist from a print background and I have lived (and died) by the mantra of CMYK. But sticking to tradition (aka "sticking your head in the sand") won't do in this ever-changing world.

When the CEO of The Economist showed me the latest gadget he picked up on his travels in the United States I was rather underwhelmed (although, rather sensibly, I didn't let it show). It was a Kindle. Ghastly, I thought. Unintuitive interface, black and white screen, dodgy keyboard and a rather blandly designed product.

But he had the vision to see that this was going to be the first of many "digital devices" that are set to rock the world of print media. That's why he's boss and I'm not.

Like those lucky women who had a short labour during childbirth, it's been a painful, but very fast transition. The Economist is now published on the Kindle, iPhone, iPad and a host of android devices. For those of us who have no idea what an android is, it's not a robot that resembles a human being, it's the name given to the operating system used on devices that aren't Apple devices. Apple has its own operating system. That's the end of any nerdy talk from me.

Despite myself, I bought an iPad recently, because I couldn't stand the intrigue any longer. And I, yes cynical old me, love it. I enjoy the freedom of downloading The Times every morning without getting out of bed; watching serialised drama (because there's always one episode I miss) on BBC iPlayer; and, of course, the best thing is images look rather fabulous on the device.

So, where does this leave illustrators in all this flurry and excitement of new media?

Some illustrators have embraced the technology. Dave Simonds, one of The Economist's regular contributors, uses ArtStudio on his iPhone to do sketches when he's out and about. He says he doesn't always have his sketch pad with him when he's travelling, but he always carries his iPhone. And it's easy to send sketches to clients from the device, rather than having to scan the rough before sending.

Others are not such big fans and find the medium gets in the way of the connection between mind, hand and paper. They are quite happy drawing woolly mammoths in their caves and I think that is fine too.

I fondly remember Ged Melling, cigarette in his mouth, with an impossibly long strip of ash dangling from it, gluing together ripped up bits of his drawings and using Tipex to create his wildly funny and ironic cartoons.

Basically, there are two ways to create an illustration: ink on paper, or pixels on a computer. I'm a big fan of both.

Although, I occasionally have work experience youngsters in the art department and when I show them one of Peter Schrank's vivid and poignant illustrations they are universally wowed by holding a 'real' piece of artwork. There is nothing quite like seeing the originality and beauty of a hand-drawn line - rather like going to a live concert.

It is this connection, so often lost in print, which comes through on the iPad. The glow and luminosity is captivating. You feel you could dive in and touch the image – every line, the depth of colour, even the paper texture is reproduced in detail. It gives humanity and personality to illustrations that defies technology.

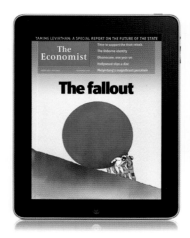

Clockwise from top:
Illustrations by
Noma Bar
Belle Mellor
Daniel Pudles
Claudio Munoz
Dave Simonds (top)
Peter Schrank (bottom)
KAL
Satoshi Kambayashi
The Ecomomist on the iPad

Obviously, artwork created on computers and viewed on the iPad also avoids the disappointment of print and is more faithful to the original. Just look at Noma Bar's illustrations on an iPad, with their swathes of flat colour, filled with meaning and menace. Unequivocally, these devices are great for showing off illustrators' work.

Can it stop at the transfer of artwork used in static print? Well, of course it can and in many cases that's for the best. But, the answer is in the word "static", because these devices are anything but. Anyone who has used a hand-held digital device wants to play– you just can't help it. It's fun. Childish, but fun.

Illustrators are naturally curious and adventurous creatures, so they won't be able to pass up a chance to explore this media. Stepping into the world of animation will be the next giant leap for print illustrators. Some are already having fun, like Daniel Pudles and Belle Mellor, whose characters come to life in their animated form. Claudio Munoz, another regular contributor to The Economist (although, a children's book illustrator by trade) visualises his work in motion. I'd love to see his cute, eccentric characters skipping across my screen. They would be perfect for children to enjoy in an electronic book.

And Kal, who often draws his political cartoons in panels, which step progressively into the political mire, would be engaging to swipe through, or see as a slide show.

Illustrations by Jorge Colombo, which were created using an iPad drawing app, are interesting and I'm sure these apps will become increasingly powerful and refined. But the tools of the trade should not determine the future of illustration. Jackson Pollock and William Turner were at each end of the visual spectrum, but it wasn't their medium that defined them, it was their vision and creativity.

When tradition meets technology there are usually trade-offs, but I have been captivated by this new medium and can only see this new digital hand-held world in a shiny, glowing light. Is it time for the AOI to come up with an app?

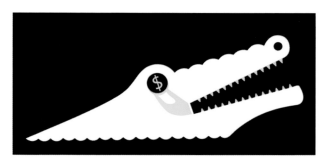

Glen McBeth
Sawney Skull

Medium Pen, ink and digital
Brief Sawney Bean was a Scottish cannibal who holed up in a cave with his wife and 14 kids - and ate passers by!
Commissioned by Susanne Frank
Client BBC History Magazine

"There are tricky subject matters (and sometimes tricky clients) and sometimes it'd be nice to have more hours in the day, more energy, several arms, two heads or a handy helper but in general it's a privilege and a lot of fun being an illustrator."

Glen McBeth has been working in illustration since graduating from Duncan of Jordanstone College of Art in Dundee in 1991. He has worked on jobs in all sectors of illustration but especially loves the challenge of a regular editorial slot. There's a new subject and challenge every week or month and Glen thinks that it's in editorial work that the illustrative personality gets nurtured.

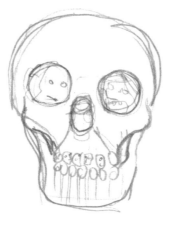

Matthew Cook
Election 2010 Interview:
David Cameron

Medium Acrylic inks and collage
Brief To draw a loose sketch of The Times Editor and Political Editor as they interview David Cameron on a train before the election, using spot colour. Deadline 9pm same day.
Commissioned by Jon Hill
Client The Times

Since graduating with a First-class Honours degree with Distinction from Kingston School of Art in 1986, **Matthew Cook**'s career has flourished with a fascinating and diverse number of commissions.

He has worked in Papua New Guinea, North Korea, Brazil, Peru, New Zealand and the United States among other countries and has undertaken many varied commissions in the UK. For example, in 1994 he illustrated five summertime stamps for the Royal Mail and, in 1999, he was commissioned to draw the hotels of The Savoy Hotel Group. Many of his projects have been for The Times for whom he has produced over ten portfolios of work. Recording life at their print works, and covering four Parliamentary elections. The All England Lawn Tennis Club secured Matthew as its first Championship Artist in 2006.

In 1991 he joined the 10th Battalion of the Parachute Regiment and then The Rifles of the Territorial Army and was War Artist for The Times in Iraq in 2003. Served in Iraq in 2004. In 2006 and 2009 he went to Afghanistan with the British Army.

Drawings in public collections:
The MoD Art Collection
The National Army Museum, Chelsea
RAF Museum, Hendon
RAF College Cranwell
3 Royal Horse Artillery
3 REME
The All England Lawn Tennis Club, Wimbledon
The Times Archive
Rothschild Bank Archive
Kingston Museum

Editorial • Bronze Award

Andrew Baker
Life After Redundancy

Medium Digital
Brief To illustrate a story in Museums Journal.
The writer talks to a few of the many people
in the museum sector who have been made
redundant to find out how they are coping.
Commissioned by Jamie Trendall
Client Esterson Associates
Commissioned for Museums Journal

Andrew Baker is an illustrator and
academic with over twenty years
experience in editorial illustration.
He studied at Liverpool Polytechnic
and the Royal College of Art, and
now teaches illustration at Middlesex
University. His illustrations have
appeared in most serious UK
newspapers and magazines, from
The Times to The Economist, and
in many design formats including
posters and book covers. His work is
regularly exhibited and he has curated
a number of group shows with other
leading British illustrators. He has
previously been awarded Gold in the
editorial section of AOI Images.

About Museums Journal:
"This commission came through Jamie
Trendall, who I worked with for many
years during his time as designer at
The Radio Times. Now at Esterson
Associates he had the opportunity to
commission bigger illustrations. The
idea for this image came instantly.
I usually have several pages of
sketches for each commission but in
this case I went straight to a rough,
and completed the work in a day or
two. The best ones sometimes seem
to come together quite effortlessly,
but behind this image is all the prior
experience of working together."

New Media • Essay
Anrick Bregman • Interactive Director, unit9

As an interactive director, Anrick creates interactive content; using technology to allow dialogue and exchange between the viewer and the story.

His work has been recognised by the leading industry institutions, and he has made creative content for organisations such as the Ministry of Health in France, Toshiba, Orange, Gotmilk?, Heinz, FedEx, Adobe, Stella Artois, and IBM, among others. Anrick worked for seven years as a animation director at Cartoon Network and MTV, writing and directing award-winning short form content. He is the founder and curator of Jolly Butcher, an art and culture webzine. And he explores and exhibits code-generated installation artwork as part of Tango & Hawaii.

Illustration in new media.

As a creator of new media content I work with illustration daily, in some form or another. The process we follow to complete a project at unit9 is often highly technical but it's very easy for that to overshadow what else goes into the work we make. At their core our projects are narrative-driven and in new media terms, illustration is a driving force for interacting with the narrative.

Although an illustration is a seemingly passive element, it can be the most active component in an interactive context. And often it is literally the foundation upon which the experience is built.

I'd like to go through three key projects of mine and talk a bit more about the process we followed, and how illustration linked in to that. In each I used illustration in a different and perhaps unconventional way.

Toshiba

For an earlier project [a project done a while ago...], I worked on a website for Toshiba, showcasing online their innovative technologies. It is a fully animated and interactive showcase for the brand, but was built on top of a single hand-drawn full-screen illustration.

At the surface, the experience is about a fantastical forest you can explore. (It has to be said that Toshiba were brave to go along with this). But lurking below the immediately obvious there is this single huge illustration; it is the forest, but also acts as the website's canvas.

And it is this image which sets up the style, the mood, and fills up the screen with infinite detail. It is what completes the big picture.

It was first worked out in pencil, then painted by hand in photoshop with a beautifully styled approach. It took as long to complete as everything else in the project combined, and was only added to the site about three days before going live.

I knew from the very beginning that this illustration would be the key element within our overall composition, and it remains the hardest working element within the site.

Attraction

Attraction is a more recent project an interactive anime commissioned by the French Ministry of Health, as part of a nation-wide anti-smoking campaign.

I worked with Koji Morimoto in Tokyo to create it, and it [the anime] combines traditional cell animation seamlessly with interactive Flash code, essentially allowing people to interact with the story by moving in front of their webcam.

It was a fairly complex build because aside from the scriptwriting, we had all the usual steps to follow when you're making an animated film. Character design, art direction, voicing, music composition etc. But we also have a super difficult technological element being added into the mix.

Animation production happened in Tokyo and interactive production in London and Italy.

And as a result of that, illustration provided me with the only way I could communicate with the Japanese Animation Director and his team, as the project grew and developed.

There was both a language barrier and a totally different skill-set dividing our two teams, and uniting them on creative and technical issues was a big challenge. To solve it we used detailed illustrations coming from both sides of the fence in a kind of illustrated dialogue.

They were used as technical breakdowns, storyboards, and - further on in the job - built into illustrated prototypes mimicking the final site, allowing the whole Japanese team to experience what they were animating before they actually did the work.

We also used illustration as a means to create interactivity while retaining a very traditional animation process.

It was essential to keep the look of traditional anime-style cell animation when building fully interactive parts of the story, rather than resort to a kind of 'cut-scene' mechanic often used in games.

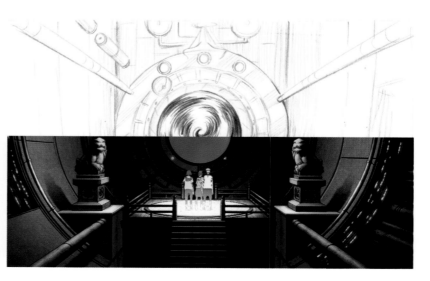

The animation team in Japan created highly detailed and layered illustrations in a traditional way, and passed those over to our interactive team, who added movement by bringing them into a coded environment and turning them into finished, reactive sequences.

It took a big leap of faith for both teams to embrace each others methods and priorities. And it took many hours of drawing to get the image to look, feel and respond just right.

Xtreme Xrunch Kart

This is a racing game I was commissioned to make by the U.S. based Carrot Farmers Association. It features a shopping kart with a rocket strapped to it, massive explosions, and heavy metal music.

It also features highly detailed hand-drawn illustrations of buildings, streets, and cars, that were wrapped round simple 3D blocks to create a richly detailed world you can drive through when playing the game.

The game is build on the 3D unity engine, which is becoming more popular on the web and mobile devices. But textures and lighting sometimes seem too smooth and perfect in 3D. Everything feels somehow perfectly calculated. What I really wanted to do was put some

imperfections in there. Some chaos.

In a toon-shading inspired approach, we combined two very different elements to make the game look just right. We created a city for the game, as highly detailed illustrations. Hand-made, a little messy. Rough around the edges the way only something hand-drawn can be.

At the same time, we made super simple 3D models. Simply shaped buildings, streets, cars, bikes, and many other objects. We then wrapped the hand-made illustrations around the 3D shapes, turning the illustrations into texture maps.

For us, wanting not to compromise on the realism of the game, this texture mapping approach allowed us to put all the detail into flat drawings, to the point where even the light coming from a window as the game turns to night is actually a detail build into the original illustration.

It's a great way to create a highly customised world, with many non-repeated details. But the shapes are just squares and rectangles, But they are beautifully rich with detail because of the illustrations wrapped around them.

Conclusion

My key point in commenting about these three projects is that the web used to be a space made by designers.

And this is opening up. Experiences online and on your mobile are more entertainment oriented, and are becoming more narrative driven.

In that sense, there is much more space for illustration to lead in New Media because, especially here at unit9, it is the foundation upon which our experiences are built.

Clockwise from top:
Xtreme Xrunch Kart: texturing work in progress and finished streetscene illustration

Attraction: prototype sketch, final animation screenshot and interactive prototype sketch

Toshiba: sketch for background and final rendering

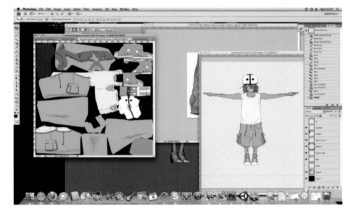

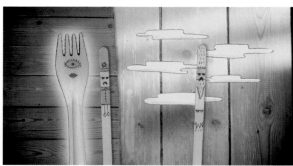

Greg McLeod
Sticks

Medium Digital and mixed media
Brief To write and produce an animated comedy series for BBC Comedy online. Animated with coffee stirrers and other wooden cutlery.
Commissioned by Martin Tricky
Client BBC

The award winning, triple BAFTA nominated **Brothers McLeod** (Greg and Myles) have a track record in creating animation for TV, web, and film. They are represented by Aardman Animations as Commercials Directors and have directed campaigns for Skittles, Stena Line, and Guinness amongst others. They have written and directed series for BBC (Pedro and Frankensheep) and Tate Galleries (Art Sparks), and written for a range of TV, Games and web projects (Noddy, SpongeBob SquarePants, NHS Relationships and Sex). They have a well established YouTube channel and have had several internet successes including Spamland and Fuggy Fuggy which was picked up by MTV and Mondo Media. In early 2009, they were nominated for a BAFTA Film Award in the Short Animation category for their film Codswallop. Late 2009, they were nominated for two BAFTA Children's Awards for their work with the Tate.

Their surname is pronounced MacCloud for those not versed in Norse-Scottish history...

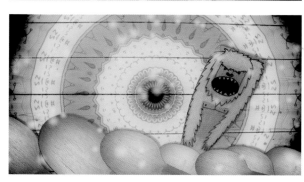

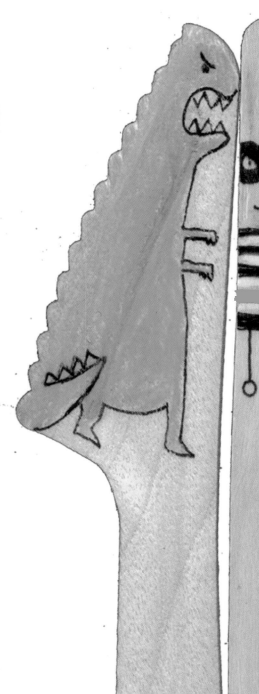

Emma Fitzgerald
How To Murder Birds

Medium Collage and digital collage
Brief Music Video for song 'How to Murder Birds' by Lupen Crook. The image provided is one of the storyboard stills that I have exhibited as an illustration.
Client Lupen Crook

Emma Fitzgerald is a collage illustrator and Stop Motion animator, living and working in London. Nominated for a D&AD Award for her animations in 2008, after graduating Emma has directed and animated music videos, designed for Marks and Spencers, animated for theatre projections, illustrated for magazines and exhibited at wonderful places, such as Wilton's Music Hall. Emma floats between disciplines and it is the attention to movement and placement in her illustrations that mark her out as an animator. Currently working on digital collages with her signature subdued colour palette and mournful feel, Emma would like to make a Stop Motion Film and illustrate book jackets of Gabriel García Márquez novels.

New Media • Bronze Award

Simon Spilsbury
Yeti

Medium Ink
Brief To create some live art for the Illustration II
exhibition at Mauger Modern Art.
Commissioned by Richard Mauger
Client Mauger Modern Art

Simon Spilsbury's work has appeared
extensively across all media for
the past 17 years. His illustration
is characterised by its energy and
its ability to communicate with
immediacy. He has a primal urge to
draw and does so at every opportunity.
He has lots of clients around the world
and has won lots of awards.

Self Promotion • Essay
Martin Colyer • Design Director, Reader's Digest Magazine

Martin Colyer has worked in magazines (since the days of hot metal) for the likes of Radio Times, The Listener, The Observer and The Sunday Times Magazine, and also helped launch Blueprint. He is currently Design Director of Reader's Digest Magazine. He has had a parallel career in music as a member of great lost Brit Soul combo Hot House, and as one of the founders of Rock's Backpages, a music journalism website.

A nostalgic anecdote. When I was starting out in magazines, the few illustrators who came out of the few art schools with illustration courses would come and see the few art directors at the few magazines that used illustration.

And you would see anyone who called, and I used to set aside a whole afternoon a week to see talented cartoonists, illustrators and painters. Their publicity material was usually a small card that they'd leave for you. You'd pin in on the noticeboard by your desk. You didn't have a computer. The only way you knew what was current was to look at other magazines, or the portfolios of the people who came to see you. No blogs, no exhibitions, no websites, no email. You knew virtually everyone in the industry, maybe with two degrees of separation.

We actually only really knew the trends in illustration in hindsight, looking at the annuals that came out eighteen months later. And they weren't necessarily a true representation of the breadth of work being done. But it was pretty much all there was.

That was then, and this is now.

Now you learn who is doing what, as instantly as any image maker wishes to make it public. The curated blogs – Creative Review, sites like Drawger, the various AOI blogs – bring the world of design and drawing to your desktop instantly and constantly.

Now you can't avoid a deluge of visual information – emailers from agents and illustration hubs arrive in inboxes unbidden and frequently.

I commission for a monthly magazine that uses about six illustrations per issue. So I'm not even a medium sized commissioner of illustration anymore and below is a my 'illustration' inbox from a typical day. All interesting and there's some great work linked to, and I barely have time to look at it all. And below is a picture of a selection of a fairly typical week's postal promos and, again, the work is often good, and some of it relevant to us, and all of it cost the illustrator time, effort and money. So to pay that back, one looks through, files away, pins up the things that work for you. And sometimes something really catches your eye and you call up and get the illustrator to bring their folio in. That's always interesting and rewarding, as you see a broader range of work, often in context, and you make some kind of personal connection, which is a vital ingredient in any commissioning relationship. So that one email or post can be the trigger for that to happen.

Over the years I have been sent great promos. The thrill of limited-edition posters arriving from the young Jonny Hannah, of beautiful and tiny origami-like books being left by Roderick Mills, of small plastic wallets filled with badges and postcards and prints from Martin O'Neill. In fact, in the new media landscape the right 'craft object' may cut through and get you commissioned.

But I think that the key is to be your own illustrator – have something that people want to come to you for, be it personality, colour, line, humour, a unique take. So, some advice:

Research. By reading the design blogs and looking about you and digging around to find the name of the person who actually looked at an image maker's work and said "This is the person to do the shop window painting or the 16 sheet poster job."

Do. A piece of work that sums up the best of what you do. Yes, I know your work has too much breadth and depth to be reduced to one image, but try. People don't have a lot of time or visual space (now that they are bombarded by images constantly) to give you.

Get technical. Find out 1) how to make small pdfs that look good 2) how to build websites or blogs that don't take too long to get to the point, show the images well and are edited down to within an inch of their lives (hire a friend to help you make the hard choices) and 3) how to embed animations in YouTube links .

Think. About who you're sending your work to, and if they are likely to use it. Focus your efforts on people who'll hire you, not on those who are never going to. Think about interesting ways to show how you are different from others and why people should hire you. It's not enough to just say "I'm here".

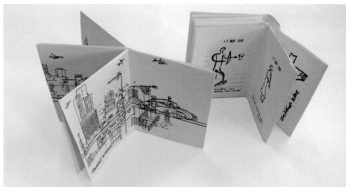

Clockwise from top:
Foldout leaflet by Richard Beards
Booklet by Roderick Mills
Cards by Jonny Hannah
Envelope by Jemma Farrow
A week's worth of postal samples
Typical daily 'illustration' inbox

Self Promotion • Gold Award

Jonny Hannah
A Bed Of Sea & Dead Men's Suits

Medium Mixed media
Brief Design a poster for my one man show at
St. Judes Gallery, Norfolk.

Jonny Hannah studied at the
Cowdenbeath College of Knowledge,
Liverpool Art School and then the
Royal College of Art. For the last
thirteen years he has been a freelance
illustrator, and is represented by the
Heart Agency. His many clients include
The Sunday Telegraph, The New York
Times and The St. Kilda Courier.

Any spare minute is spent working
on new projects for his own Cakes
& Ale Press, busily creating books,
posters, prints and occasionally
t-shirts, ready to exhibit here and there,
including St. Jude's in Sunny Norfolk.

Melvyn Evans
The Worry

Medium Linoprint
Brief The character in the story carries a worry in a bag, but has forgotten why he has the worry. Eventually he looses the bag and therefore the worry.

1985-87 Exeter College of Art and Design

1987-88 Coldsmiths College, London

1991-93 Studied drawing at the Royal College of Art (Professor Bryan Kneale RA).

1991 Joined New Division Illustration Agency

2005 Finalist in the "Transport for London" competition, the artwork was used for promoting and advertising the award event at the London Transport Museum.

Commissions include work for Vodaphone, Halifax Building Society advertising campaign, packaging for Waitrose and Marks and Spencer, Mini Cooper promotional material, and Network Southeast poster campaign.
   'Visible Voices' a poetry anthology for Channel4, 'Positive Business' a series of books for Duncan Baird and cookery books by Amy Wilcock for Ebury Press.

He had forgotten why he carried a worry in his bag

Self Promotion • Bronze Award

Jill Calder
Forest Deer

Medium Digital and mixed media
Brief Create an image that illustrates the word
"Edge". The Edge of the Forest seemed like a
good place to start...

Based in Fife, Scotland, **Jill Calder**
has been working as an illustrator
since 1993. She is also a calligrapher,
painter, digital artist and lecturer with
a love of drawing, ideas, colour, ink,
typography, book-binding, sketchbooks
and yes, deadlines. Jill aims to
combine traditional and digital image-
making methods as seamlessly as
possible to create her illustrations.
    Her clients come to her from both
the UK and much further afield and
include Visa, The New Yorker, Adobe,
Penguin, Siemens, Crusaid and a
snail farm in in the West Highlands
of Scotland.

SELECTED WORKS

Each entry is marked by the jury according to how well the work fulfils the brief, originality, and technical ability. Only the highest scoring images are invited to feature in the annual.

Peter Strain
Trying To Poke A Hole In The World
Category Self Promotion
Medium Pen and ink, coloured digitally
Brief Create an image that depicts people from
various walks of life struggling to make their mark.

Sarah Coleman
The Natural History Museum
Category Design
Medium Ink
Brief Create an illustration for range of own-branded gift items for the the NHM; it had to summarise the 9 million or so amazing, diverse objects in the museum in one image!
Commissioned by Craig Manley
Client The Natural History Museum

45rpm
Category Design
Medium Ink
Brief Originally created for the twin roles of promotional t-shirt for Factoryroad, UK manufacturers of 45rpm adapters, and as a response to an editorial challenge by Computer Arts Magazine.
Commissioned by Leigh Adams and Nick Carson
Client Factoryroad and Computer Arts

David Dean
Johnny Swanson
Category Children's Books
Medium Acrylic
Brief The cover should look like a newspaper from 1929 (to fit with the story). Monochrome seemed a bit bland for a children's book, so I introduced a number of colour objects to sit "on" the newspaper.
Commissioned by Alison Gadsby
Client David Fickling Books

Tall Story
Category Children's Books
Medium Acrylic
Brief The brief was fairly open. The book is about an 8 foot tall boy who arrives from the Philippines to live with his family in London. The cover needed to reflect all of these elements.
Commissioned by Alison Gadsby
Client David Fickling Books

Christopher Gibbs
The Time Machine
Category Books
Medium Digital
Brief To illustrate the paperback cover of The Time Machine by H G Wells for Gollanz's Masterworks Series.
Commissioned by
Sue Michniewicz
Client Orion Publishing
Commissioned for
Gollanz Masterworks

Rod Hunt
Where's Stig?
The World Tour - New York
Category Books
Medium Digital
Brief Find the mysterious Stig.
Create New York for Where's Stig?
The World Tour, referencing the
BBC TV show Top Gear.
Commissioned by Charlie Turner
Client Top Gear
Commissioned for BBC Books

Where's Stig?
The World Tour - Monaco
Category Books
Medium Digital
Brief Find the mysterious Stig.
Create the Monaco Grand Prix
for the book Where's Stig?
The World tour, referencing the
TV show Top Gear.
Commissioned by Charlie Turner
Client Top Gear
Commissioned for BBC Books

Where's Stig?
The World Tour – Blackpool
Category Books
Medium Digital
Brief Find the mysterious Stig.
Create Blackpool for Where's Stig?
The World Tour, referencing the
Blackpool illuminations episode
of the TV show Top Gear.
Commissioned by Charlie Turner
Client Top Gear
Commissioned for BBC Books

Where's Stig?
The World Tour – London
Category Books
Medium Digital
Brief Find the mysterious Stig.
Create London for Where's Stig?
The World Tour referencing the
London Race episode of the TV
show Top Gear.
Commissioned by Charlie Turner
Client Top Gear
Commissioned for BBC Books

Marcella Wylie
Floral Leopard
Category Self Promotion
Medium Mixed media
Brief A mixed media piece created using
photography, ink and pen. This is a portfolio
image I created for myself.

>

Staffan Gnosspelius
Sceptic
Category Children's Books
Medium Reduction wood-cut
Brief To illustrate 'the gift of the magi'
for a picture-book.
Commissioned by Hemin Yoon
Client AgaWorld Co.Ltd, South Korea

Letting The Hair Down
Category Children's Books
Medium Reduction wood-cut
Brief To illustrate the story 'the gift of the
magi' for a picture book.
Commissioned by Hemin Yoon
Client AgaWorld Co.Ltd, South Korea

Tony Simpson
Dog Warden
Category Self Promotion
Medium Pencil, paint and digital
Brief Humorous image to illustrate
canine misdemeanor.

Norwegian Wood
Category Self Promotion
Medium Digital and mixed media
Brief To create an image suggested by Haruki
Murakami's novel, Norwegian Wood.

Andrew Tudor
Poltergeist Biro
Category Self Promotion
Medium Pencil
Brief Self promotional.

Go for 60 minutes a day
Get moving, look good, feel great!

British Heart Foundation

Andy Smith
60 Minutes
Category Advertising
Medium Digital
Brief Create a poster that shows some of
the different activities that young people can
get involved in that will contribute to their
recommended 60 minutes of exercise a day.
Commissioned by Marc Atkinson
Client Marc and Anna
Commissioned for BHF

The Hot Dog
Category Design
Medium Screenprint
Brief Create a limited edition poster to
accompany a short comic strip called
The Hot Dog published by Art Bureau.
Commissioned by Bert Benson
Client Art Bureau

Liam Derbyshire
Pencil Vault
Category Editorial
Medium Digital and mixed media
Brief Illustrate an article explaining how skills in literacy were failing some people on the path to higher earnings.
Commissioned by Keval Joshi
Client The Times Educational Supplement

GTC Spying
Category Editorial
Medium Digital and mixed media
Brief Illustrate an article explaining how many teachers believed that the General Teaching Council's (GTC) code of conduct, intruded too much into their personal lives.
Commissioned by Keval Joshi
Client The Times Educational Supplement

>
Liam Bardsley
Office Party
Category Self Promotion
Medium Digital
Brief Communicating the sense of making a fool of yourself whilst being watched by others at an office party.

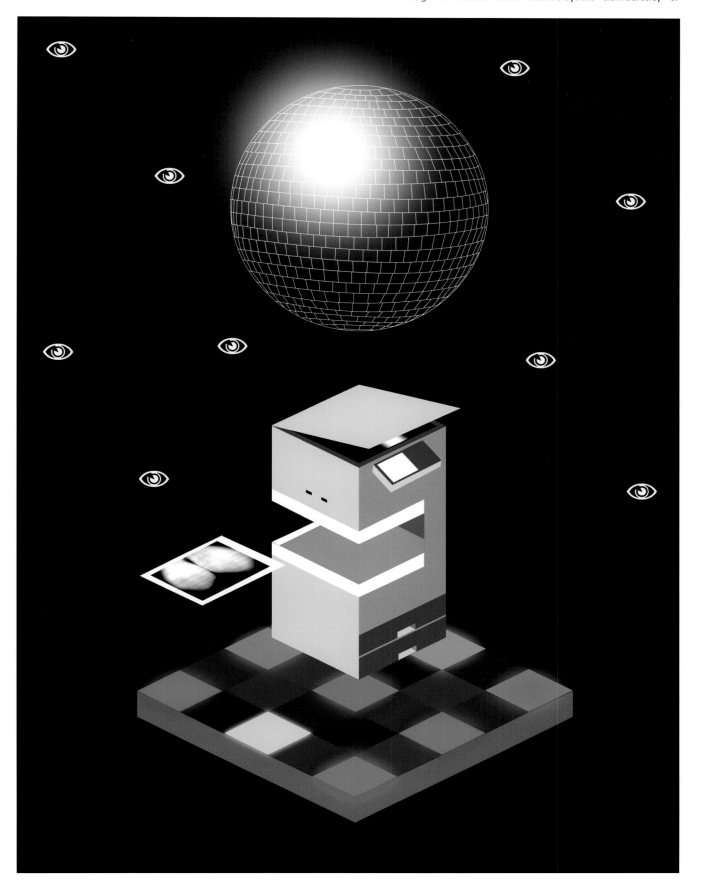

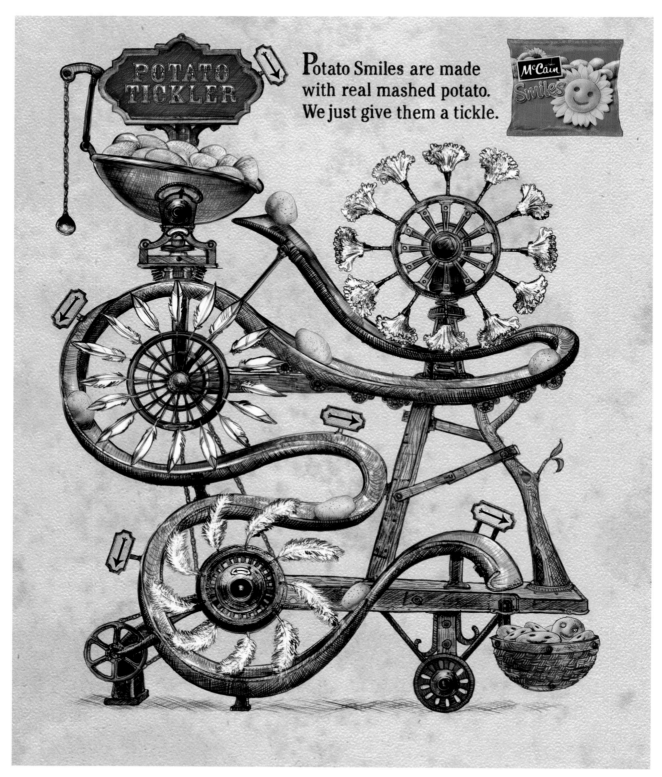

Potato Smiles are made with **real mashed potato**. We just give them a tickle.

Max Ellis
Tickle Machine
Category Advertising
Medium Ink and digital
Brief Create what looks like a mad scientists design drawing of a machine that tickles potatoes into potato smiles.
Commissioned by Julia Martens
Client Beattie McGuinness Bungay Ltd
Commissioned for McCains

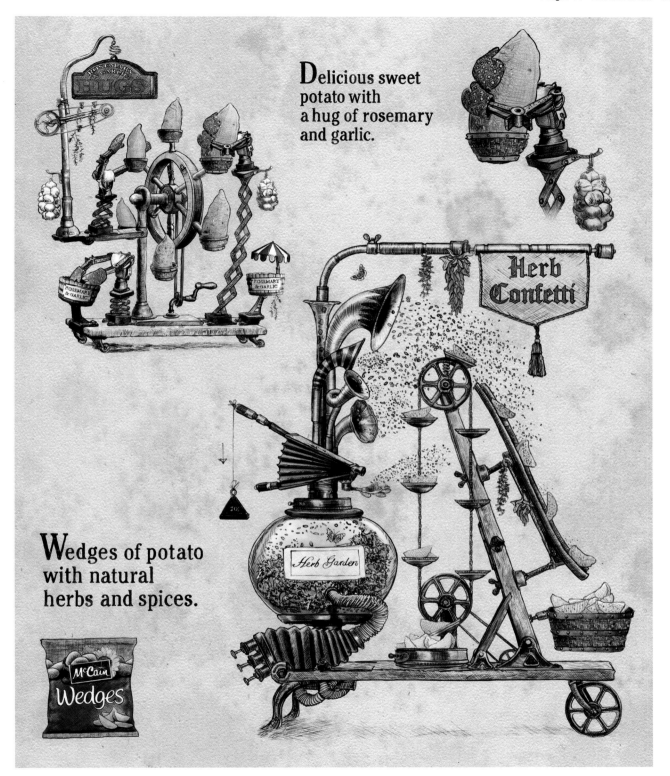

Delicious sweet potato with a hug of rosemary and garlic.

Wedges of potato with natural herbs and spices.

Sweet Potato Hugs / Herb Confetti Machine
Category Advertising
Medium Ink and digital
Brief Create a mad professors design for hugging herbs and spices onto sweet potato. Also create what looks like a mad scientist's design drawing of a machine that puffs herbs at potato wedges.
Commissioned by Julia Martens
Client Beattie McGuinness Bungay Ltd
Commissioned for McCains

Satoshi Kambayashi
Big Fish
Category Editorial
Medium Digital and mixed media
Brief The problem of Icesave (bank) was the imbalance of two nations. It was owned and backed by a small country (Iceland), while its main customers were from a far bigger nation (the UK).
Commissioned by Andrew Tod
Client The Guardian

Liberate Cannabis
Category Editorial
Medium Digital and mixed media
Brief Cannabis should be legalised.
Commissioned by Andrew Tod
Client The Guardian

BP's Problems
Category Editorial
Medium Digital and mixed media
Brief Stopping the oil leak is only the beginning, as BP faces problems from all sides.
Commissioned by Penny Garrett
Client The Economist

Nuclear Reaction
Category Editorial
Medium Digital and mixed media
Brief The word 'nuclear' triggers automatic panic reaction, but nuclear power is much safer than commonly assumed.
Commissioned by Andrew Tod
Client The Guardian

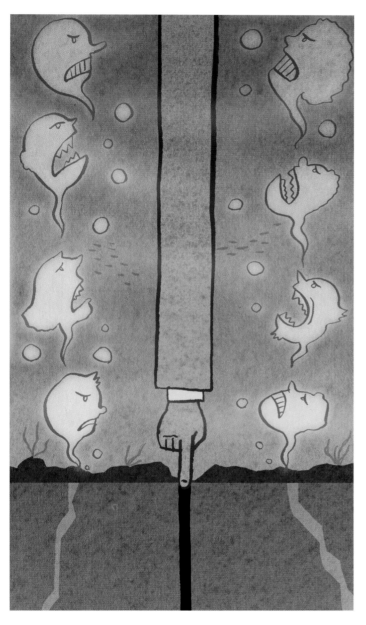

Satoshi Kambayashi
Coppélia
Category Self Promotion
Medium Digital and mixed media
Brief Create an image for Coppélia, a comic ballet where a man falls in love with an automaton/doll.

La Tour Risquée
Category Self Promotion
Medium Digital and mixed media
Brief The French have always been a bit more daring.

Charles Williams
Nike Ribbons
Category Advertising
Medium Digital
Brief The brief for this piece was to explore the Nike logotype using a geometric approach. I was given free reign in terms of what I could do with the brand mark (I don't often hear that), as long as it still conveyed the brand effectively. I chose this style as I wanted to create a dynamic, almost chaotic piece, that also had an underlying sense of order.
Commissioned by Jeff Wertz
Client Nike

Lunchboxheart
I Hope
Category Self Promotion
Medium Digital
Brief 'I Hope' was thought of as an inside
illustration that would be able to translate well into
a mounted format on a gallery wall, PVC banner or
a print on textiles for that matter.

Sam Findlay
Organic Pigs
Category Editorial
Medium Ink and computer colour
Brief This picture was commissioned for an article
about organic pig farming and the ironic twist that
it didn't matter how good a pigs life was it was still
going to be eaten!
Commissioned by Jessica Mitchell
Client The Food Magazine

They taste much better if
you let them run around

Jessie Ford
Joy Is The Best Make-Up
Category Design
Medium Digital and mixed media
Brief To create a series of typographic posters for
a poster and greetings card company in Paris.
This is one of them.
Commissioned by Dominique Seckler
Client Nouvelle Images

The Magic Of Reading
Category Editorial
Medium Digital and mixed media
Brief One of a series created over the last year for a
French Parenting Magazine, to illustrate the joy that
reading brings to children.
Commissioned by Odile Fruchart-Garcia
Client Maquette Parents
Commissioned for Parenting Magazine, Paris

A-B And All The Sights In Betweenn
Category Self Promotion
Medium Digital and mixed media
Brief To create an image promoting cycling in London.

Brian Grimwood
Art Of Italy
Category Editorial
Medium Digital and mixed media
Brief Illustrate a piece about the art of Italy.
Commissioned by Mark Lazenby
Client The World of Interiors

Hearty Eggs
Category Design
Medium Digital and mixed media
Brief Produce a Hearty egg logo made of hearts.
Commissioned by Jeremy Dicker
Client Company X Creative
Commissioned for Hearty Eggs

Spooky Spider
Category Self Promotion
Medium Digital and mixed media
Brief To enjoy drawing.

Hva Skjer I
Category Advertising
Medium Digital and mixed media
Brief Paint a face.
Commissioned by Morten Saether
Client LOX AS

He gave the duck a nice hot bath and a cup of tea.

He took down his
Enormous Book of Incredibly
Interesting Things,

he looked under 'D',

and he made a list...

'I want a pet with **PERSONALITY**. I want a Dog.

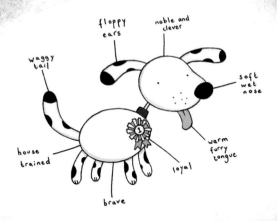

noble and
clever

floppy
ears

waggy
tail

soft
wet
nose

house
trained

warm
furry
tongue

loyal

brave

With floppy ears and a waggy tail,
and a soft wet nose, and a warm furry tongue.

'A dog that can catch
balls that I throw,

and that can learn
fantastic new tricks,

— SHAVSHIDGES

and that I can chase around trees.

Because it is common knowledge,' said Henry,
'that a dog is The Perfect Pet for a boy.'

Fiona Roberton
Wanted: The Perfect Pet
Category Children's Books
Medium Ink, gouache and charcoal
Brief Spread for the children's book
'Wanted: The Perfect Pet'.
Client Penguin

Gill Bradley
Portobello Map
Category Design
Medium Digital
Brief Illustrate a map of Portobello
Road to be printed on a linen tea
towel for sale at and to promote
Ceramica Blue. To put across the
flavor of the area and have a retro
but contemporary feel.
Commissioned by Lindy Wiffen
Client Ceramica Blue

Michael Hutchinson
We Can't Rewind
Category Self Promotion
Medium Digital
Brief Theme was Primitive. The idea is of an image forming from an audio cassette, now a primitive form of music output. The theory of Evolution is used as a reflection of how far music output has evolved.

>

Julia Woolf
The Chicken Song
Category Children's Books
Medium Digital and mixed media
Brief Illustrate a poem to teach children English.
Commissioned by Younghwa Kim
Client Korea Hermannhesse

Christmas Card
Category Self Promotion
Medium Digital
Brief Self promotion.

Garry Parsons
Dr Hoof
Category Children's Books
Medium Acrylic
Brief Dr Hoof moves to a one horse town and that one horse was Dr Hoof. Will he learn that friendship is the best medicine of all? Illustrations for a text by Diana Kimpton.
Commissioned by Emily Bannister
Client Scholastic Children's Books

The Big Freeze
Category Editorial
Medium Digital and mixed media
Brief Frances Lynn's Ironman training doesn't stop when the big freeze takes hold this winter.
Commissioned by Marco Crisari
Client NatMag Rodale
Commissioned for Triathlete's World

Garry Parsons
Magic Carpet
Category Advertising
Medium Digital and mixed media
Brief Capture the magic of children's literature across the ages. Publicity for the annual children's book award appearing on posters, advertising literature, banners, bookmarks and the web.
Commissioned by Sinead Kromer
Client Red House
Commissioned for
The Red House Children's Book Award 2010

Chicken World
Category Children's Books
Medium Digital and mixed media
Brief A humorous fast-paced thriller that is packed with all the fun of the fair! Can Franklyn evade the crafty fox amongst the chaos of the attractions? Illustrations for a text by Sean Taylor.
Commissioned by Natascha Biebow
Client Random House Children's Books

T.S Spookytooth
Robot (1304)
Category Self Promotion
Medium Digital and mixed media
Brief A self promotional piece based around
an idea for a short story, that allowed me to
experiment with painting and digital effects.

<

Gail Armstrong
Kleenex - Yes And No
Category Advertising
Medium Paper sculpture
Brief Made entirely from paper, the reflected image portrays potential outcomes of saying Yes or No to marriage. For the "Feelings" campaign showing how Kleenex is there for the good and the bad.
Commissioned by Christiano Neves
Client JWT Ltd
Commissioned for Kleenex

Keith Robinson
Penny And The Pirates
Category Children's Books
Medium Watercolour
Brief Illustrate a scene that works as a book cover and a set of 3 stamps. Each stamp perforation 'frames' one of the red-sailed boats, acting like a comic strip and creating a sense of sequential movement.
Commissioned by Dawn Gallienne
Client Guernsey Post

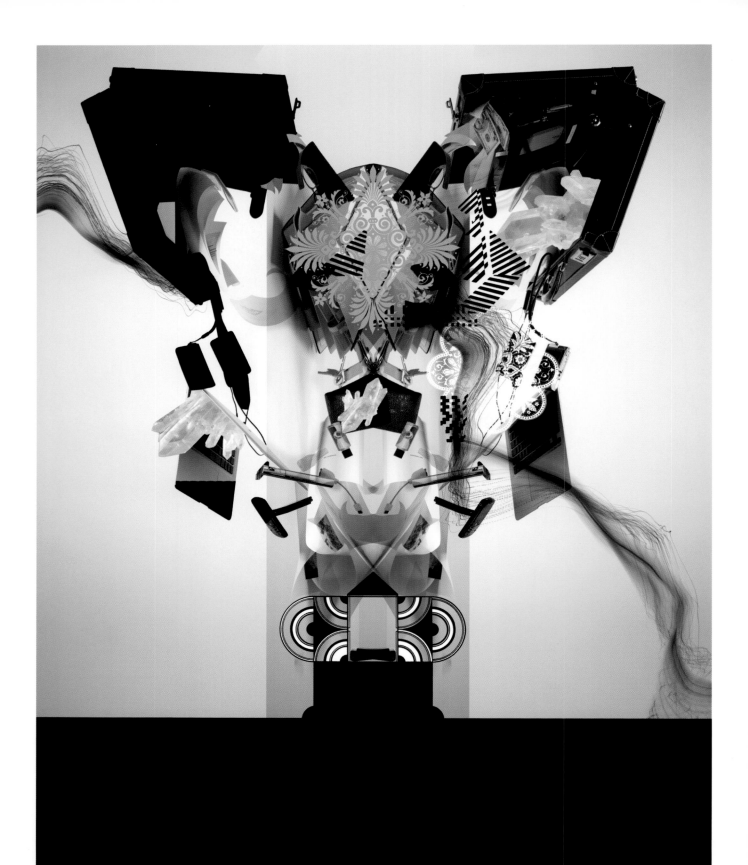

Joel Lardner
The Krystal World 0.1
Category Self Promotion
Medium Digital and mixed media
Brief The Krystal World is a collaborative project initiated by Illustrator Joel Lardner and photographer Dan Tobin Smith.

The Queen Of Spades - Harmony
Category Self Promotion
Medium Ink
Brief Based on Alexander Pushkin's short story 'The Queen of Spades'. The story is set in 19th century St.Petersburg and concerns the destructive nature of obsession.

The Queen Of Spades - The Officer
Category Self Promotion
Medium Ink
Brief Based on Alexander Pushkin's short story 'The Queen of Spades'. The story is set in 19th century St.Petersburg and concerns the destructive nature of obsession.

Joel Lardner
The Krystal World 0.2
Category Self Promotion
Medium Digital and mixed media
Brief The Krystal World is a collaborative
project initiated by Illustrator Joel Lardner
and photographer Dan Tobin Smith.

Joanne Young
Alphabet Of Caught Fish
Category Self Promotion
Medium Watercolour
Brief Create an alphabet
which explores the theme
of 'Caught Fish'.

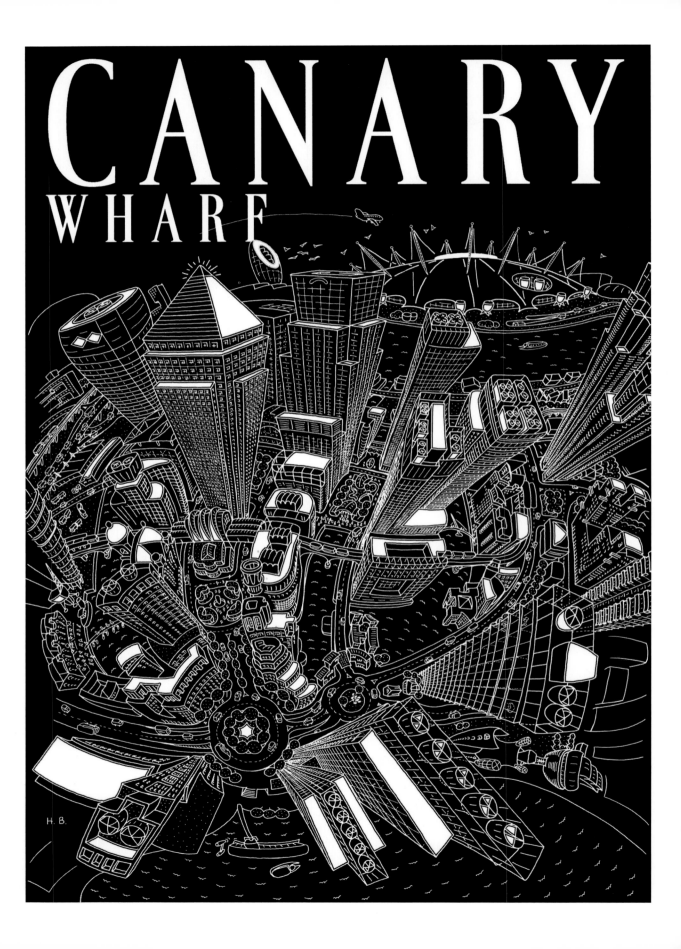

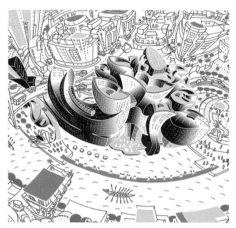
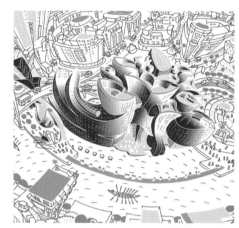

Arty Globe by Hartwig Braun
Canary Wharf Magazine Cover (July 2010)
Category Design
Medium Hand-drawn and coloured digitally
Brief Illustration of Canary Wharf for use on 'Canary Wharf' magazine cover to celebrate its 60th edition in July 2010. Printed on black with silver foil fills.
Commissioned by Giles Ellwood
Client Runwild Media Group

Guggenheim Bilbao Meets Warhol
Category Design
Medium Hand-drawn and coloured digitally
Brief To create an illustration of the Guggenheim Museum on the backdrop of Bilbao for own-brand prints and merchandise range selling at the museum shop.
Commissioned by The Buyers
Client Guggenheim Museum Bilbao

Roma
Category Design
Medium All line drawing is hand-drawn and coloured digitally
Brief To depict an iconic and easily recognisable view of Rome as a greeting card design.
Commissioned by Julia Woodmansterne
Client Woodmansterne Publications Limited

Freddy Boo
Addicted To Social Networking Sites
Category Self Promotion
Medium Digital
Brief Created in response to the rise of young
people who are addicted to social networking sites.

Rock N Roll Busker
Category Self Promotion
Medium Digital
Brief Illustration created from a sketch of a lively
busker on the Piccadilly Circus tube station.

>
Osmand Nosse
Not A Pipe
Category Self Promotion
Medium Digital and mixed media
Brief Self promotion.

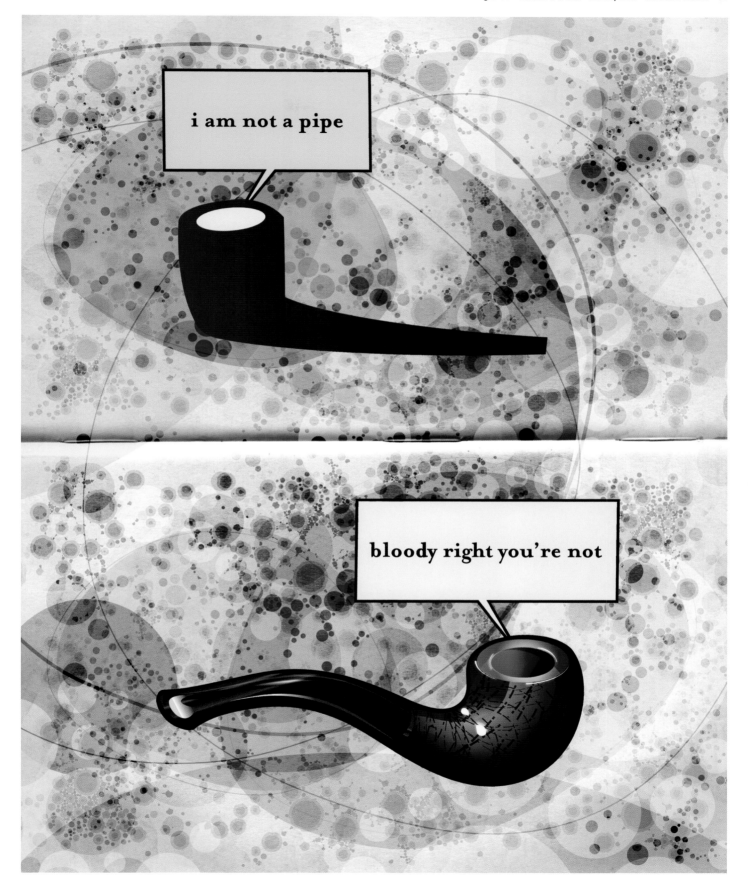

Rob Gill
On Restricted Duty? Come Back To Work... But Bring Your Stapler.
Category Self Promotion
Medium Digital and mixed media
Brief The article discussed Greater Manchester Police asking Officers on restricted duty to staple questionnaires to wage slips. However, Officer's had to provide their own staplers...

Why Is It All Quiet On The Extraterrestrial Front?
Category Self Promotion
Medium Digital and mixed media
Brief The article, taken from a daily newspaper, asks; How come nobody talks about extraterrestrials anymore?

>
Tom Morgan-Jones
Peter Cook
Category Self Promotion
Medium Ink
Brief I'm a great fan of Peter Cook and the Dagenham Dialogues, here's a bit of both.

WHENEVER I feel ill, you know, I get a dose of the flu of something I say a little prayer. I say, 'Dear God in heaven, if you're there heed my prayer. If you're not there, don't take any notice. But if you are, make me better by Tuesday at twelve o'clock and I'll know you've done it and I promise to be good for ever more and believe in you.' Of course the trouble is, when you get better you don't know whether it's because God's done it or whether you would have got better in any case.

Words P.Cook

ink TM-J

Peter Ellis
Daniel Craig
Category Self Promotion
Medium Digital and mixed media
Brief To produce a caricature of Daniel Craig
as James Bond.

Caricature Of Michael Caine
Category Editorial
Medium Digital and mixed media
Brief To produce a caricature of Michael Caine with
relevance to him appearing on Desert Island Discs.
Commissioned by Ped Millichamp
Client BBC Magazines
Commissioned for Radio Times

Carolyn Gowdy
**'Heart Trapeze', 'Everyday Life Productions,
This Moment Is Filled With Now!'**
Category Self Promotion
Medium Mixed media
Brief Part of ongoing 'Life is an Adventure,
Life is a Gift' series.

'Dreamboat', 'Live As If Heaven Is On Earth'
Category Self Promotion
Medium Mixed media
Brief Part of ongoing 'Life is an Adventure,
Life is a Gift' series.

'The Dreams Of Bethany Mellmoth'
Category Editorial
Medium Mixed media
Brief For humorous short story by William Boyd.
Strong feelings are triggered for Bethany Mellmoth.
She was only 4 years old when her father walked
out on Christmas Day. Is it time to take revenge?
Commissioned by Mary Wakefield
Client The Spectator Magazine, Christmas Issue

'Wake Up Call', 'Tree Of Life'
Category Books
Medium Mixed media
Brief To supply material from the various sketch,
scrapbooks I've created over the years. These two
images are part of an ongoing series entitled
'Life is an Adventure, Life is a Gift'.
Commissioned by Steve Heller
Client Thames & Hudson
Commissioned for Graphic: Inside the Sketchbooks
of the World's Great Graphic Designers

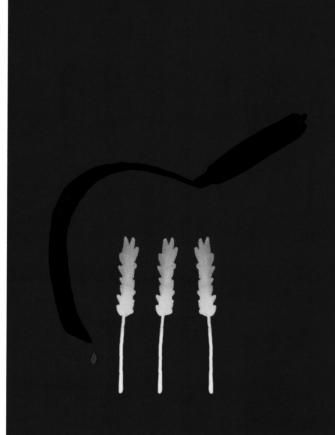

Rachel Tudor Best
The Glass Mountain
Category Design
Medium Digital and mixed media
Brief Design a set of A4 illustrations for a
Kamishibai Storyteller, depicting key scenes from
the traditional polish folktale "The Glass Mountain".
Commissioned by Elizabeth Pimblett
Client Herefordshire Council
Commissioned for
Museum Resource and Learning Centre

Hesiod's Calendar
Category Books
Medium Digital and mixed media
Brief Produce a design that suggests the two uses
of the sickle, as a weapon of the Gods, and as a
tool for farming.
Commissioned by Judith Wilson
Client Carcanet Press

Stanley Chow
Welcome To Manchester
Category Self Promotion
Medium Digital
Brief Illustrate a cityscape based on Manchester
City Centre, aimed at young children but also
appeal to parents of all ethnicities. Initially
commissioned by Manchester City Council.

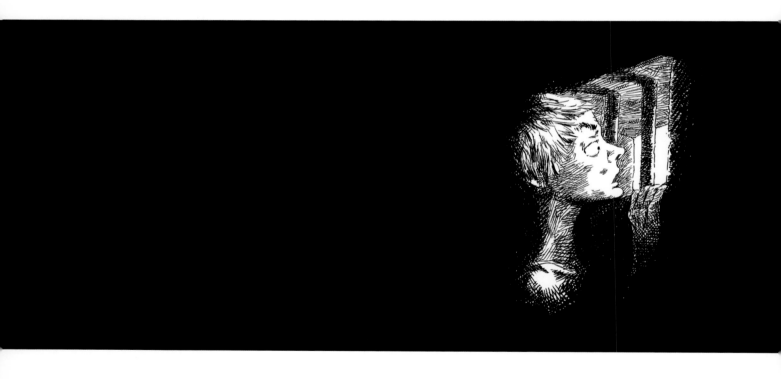

James de la Rue
Decimus Sees The Hanged Children
Category Children's Books
Medium Digital and ink
Brief Interior illustration for Gladiator Boy (book 14)
written by David Grimstone.
Commissioned by Laura Richardson
Client Hodder Children's Books

Battle Ensues
Category Children's Books
Medium Ink
Brief Interior illustration for Gladiator Boy (book 12)
written by David Grimstone.
Commissioned by Laura Richardson
Client Hodder Children's Books

Stephen Garrett
The Inky Blues
Category Self Promotion
Medium Acrylic and ink
Brief A personal project for an exhibition in Take 5 Studios London.

Banjo Joe
Category Self Promotion
Medium Acrylic and ink
Brief A personal project for an exhibition in Take 5 Studios London.

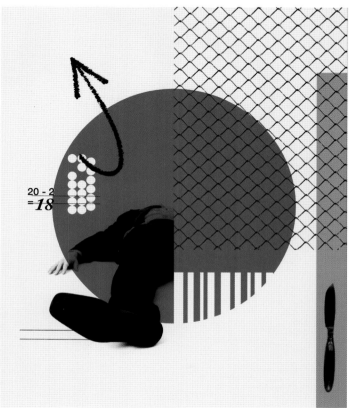

Cristiana Couceiro
The Human Connection
Category Editorial
Medium Digital
Brief Global connectivity has shifted the
definition of community towards individuals
with shared interests regardless of physical
location. Do we have too much connectivity
and not enough connection?
Commissioned by Becci Neal
Client Fortune Street
Commissioned for Research World Magazine

Me & Mr. Rafferty
Category Editorial
Medium Digital
Brief Short story by Lee Child, about the special
relationship between a serial killer and the cop
investigating the crimes.
Commissioned by Chrissy Mouncey
Client The Sunday Times

Becky Brown
Fox
Category Self Promotion
Medium Mixed media
Brief As part of my MA Illustration course I experimented with taking my drawing skills into 3D. It was important to retain a sense of character, movement and energy as well as incorporating drawn elements.

Travelling Circus
Category Self Promotion
Medium Mixed media
Brief This whole piece is a large pop up and was created as part of my experiments in 3D whilst studying on my MA in Illustration. I like the idea of worlds contained hidden within objects.

Arlene Adams
Welcome
Category Self Promotion
Medium Digital
Brief Self initiated piece.

See The World
Category Self Promotion
Medium Digital
Brief Self initiated piece.

Richard Yot
Paper Peter
Category Self Promotion
Medium Digital
Brief An image from a self-penned story, used for self-promotion and submission to publishers.

Fishing Accident
Category Self Promotion
Medium Digital
Brief The front page to my illustration website.

'TAYLOR HAS CREATED A MARVELLOUS, JUMP-OFF-THE-PAGE CHARACTER...A GENUINE SUCCESS THAT ADMIRERS OF JOHN IRVING WILL SURELY ENJOY'
THE INDEPENDENT

Meet Early "Trenchmouth" Taggart, a man born and orphaned in 1903: a one time inventor, snake handler, cunnilinguist, sniper, woodsman, harmonica man, and newspaperman. His is an epic story, a tall tale in the tradition of Mark Twain, chronicling more than one hundred years of exile and outrunning trouble. It is the love song of an outlaw and, like the best ballads, it etches its mark deep upon the memory.

'THAT RARE CREATURE – A LITERARY PAGE-TURNER – PROVES THERE'S STILL PASSION, FIRE AND BRILLIANCE IN THE AMERICAN NOVEL'
HOUSTON CHRONICLE

'WILDLY INVENTIVE'
THE TIMES

'OFTEN FUNNY, FREQUENTLY DRAMATIC AND GENUINELY TOUCHING...HE [TAYLOR] WILL BE WORTH PURSUING WHEREVER HIS TALENTS TAKE HIM'
CANBERRA TIMES

Cover design layout © HarperCollins Publishers 2010
Cover illustration by David Bromley

FSC + HarperCollins
Sustainable reading
www.harpercollins.co.uk/green
Your choice makes a difference

LOVE THIS BOOK? WWW.BOOKARMY.COM

UK £7.99* ISBN 978-0-00-733954-9
*recommended price
9 780007 339549

THE BALLAD OF TRENCHMOUTH TAGGART
GLENN TAYLOR

blue door

GLENN TAYLOR

THE BALLAD OF TRENCHMOUTH TAGGART

'A GALLOPING, DEFIANT EPIC...A VIRTUOSO PERFORMANCE' THE GUARDIAN

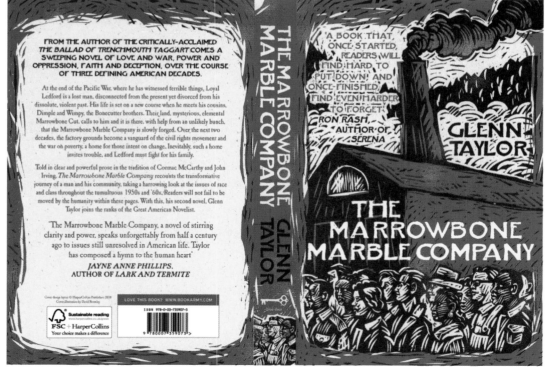

FROM THE AUTHOR OF THE CRITICALLY-ACCLAIMED THE BALLAD OF TRENCHMOUTH TAGGART COMES A SWEEPING NOVEL OF LOVE AND WAR, POWER AND OPPRESSION, FAITH AND DECEPTION, OVER THE COURSE OF THREE DEFINING AMERICAN DECADES.

At the end of the Pacific War, where he has witnessed terrible things, Loyal Ledford is a lost man, disconnected from the present yet divorced from his dissolute, violent past. His life is set on a new course when he meets his cousins, Dimple and Wimpy, the Bonecutter brothers. Their land, mysterious, elemental Marrowbone Cut, calls to him and it is there, with help from an unlikely bunch, that the Marrowbone Marble Company is slowly forged. Over the next two decades, the factory grounds become a vanguard of the civil rights movement and the war on poverty, a home for those intent on change. Inevitably, such a home invites trouble, and Ledford must fight for his family.

Told in clear and powerful prose in the tradition of Cormac McCarthy and John Irving, The Marrowbone Marble Company recounts the transformative journey of a man and his community, taking a harrowing look at the issues of race and class throughout the tumultuous 1950s and '60s. Readers will not fail to be moved by the humanity within these pages. With this, his second novel, Glenn Taylor joins the ranks of the Great American Novelist.

'The Marrowbone Marble Company, a novel of stirring clarity and power, speaks unforgettably from half a century ago to issues still unresolved in American life. Taylor has composed a hymn to the human heart'
JAYNE ANNE PHILLIPS,
AUTHOR OF LARK AND TERMITE

Cover design layout © HarperCollins Publishers 2010
Cover illustration by David Bromley

FSC + HarperCollins
Sustainable reading
Your choice makes a difference

LOVE THIS BOOK? WWW.BOOKARMY.COM

ISBN 978-0-00-735907-3
9 780007 359073

THE MARROWBONE MARBLE COMPANY
GLENN TAYLOR

'A BOOK THAT, ONCE STARTED, READERS WILL FIND HARD TO PUT DOWN, AND ONCE FINISHED, FIND EVEN HARDER TO FORGET'
RON RASH, AUTHOR OF SERENA

GLENN TAYLOR

THE MARROWBONE MARBLE COMPANY

David Bromley
The Ballad Of Trenchmouth Taggart
Category Books
Medium Linocut and digital
Brief The image had to have a woodcut rawness reflecting the backwoodsman lifestyle of the main character.
Commissioned by Nick Shah
Client HarperCollins

The Marrowbone Marble Company
Category Books
Medium Linocut and digital
Brief The publishers wanted an image that was a rough woodcut, with a feeling of austerity, reflecting hard post war life in West Virginia.
Commissioned by Nick Shah
Client HarperCollins

A.Richard Allen
Brat Farrar (Chapter 4)
Category Books
Medium Digital and mixed media
Brief A plate for the Folio Society's edition of the 1940s thriller, Brat Farrar. The caption here is, 'Oh! Sorry!' he said at once. 'Thought you were a friend of-' And then he stopped and stared.
Commissioned by Sheri Gee
Client The Folio Society

Brat Farrar (Chapter 29)
Category Books
Medium Digital and mixed media
Brief A plate for the Folio Society's edition of the 1940s thriller, Brat Farrar. The caption here is, 'He expelled his breath in a whispered laugh. 'A sheer drop to the ground, half a hillside away'.
Commissioned by Sheri Gee
Client The Folio Society

>
Fossil Glanville
See London Cycling
Category Self Promotion
Medium Digital
Brief Self promotional poster to encourage cycling as a means of transport in London.

Heather Horsley
Roadside Cafes
Category Self Promotion
Medium Digital, mixed media and monoprint
Brief To produce a book commenting on elements relating to the British roadside cafe culture and environment. An exploration of the connections between person, product and place.

Usual Customers
Category Self Promotion
Medium Digital, mixed media and monoprint
Brief To produce a book commenting on elements relating to the British roadside cafe culture and environment. An exploration of the connections between person, product and place.

>
Christiane Engel
Locals Only - London
Category Self Promotion
Medium Acrylics on wood and digital collage
Brief Participating Society 6 artists were asked to create a visual examination of the place they call home.

Alice Tait
British Bats
Category Self Promotion
Medium Pencil and inks
Brief I was initially only briefed to do a couple of bats for Heritage Today but had so much fun with them that I carried on drawing to produce this self promotional illustration for my website.
Commissioned by Helen Little
Client Seven Publishing

Woodland Mushrooms
Category Books
Medium Pencil and inks
Brief One of a series of full page illustrations for 'Good Things' by Jane Grigson. I drew from life to create this scene, inspired by the writer's cookery recipes from English and French farmhouses.
Commissioned by Sheri Gee
Client The Folio Society

Zanny Mellor
Drink It Up
Category Self Promotion
Medium Digital and mixed media
Brief This is my very optimistic expression
of the importance of friendships. The glass
is definitely more than half full!

Beat The Rush
Category Self Promotion
Medium Digital and mixed media
Brief Responding to the London Transport
Museum and AOI's 'Cycling in London'
competition about the benefits of cycling
in London and how it can be a quicker
way to commute.

Beugism
We Have Come A Long Way
Category Self Promotion
Medium Acrylic
Brief For my personal project called "A Nest Box Formerly Known As Home" - I use birds as alter egos in order to deal with issues like death, love and alienation from home.

Hiroshi Kariya
Tiger Tate Thunder
Category Self Promotion
Medium Mixed media
Brief This image is designed to be silk-screen printed for entering to the "Release" competition held by the Tate and CultureLabel in 2010. A main concept is celebrating for Tate and Tiger year of 2010.

Thunder Fighter
Category Self Promotion
Medium Mixed media
Brief This image was designed to be silk-screen printed as part of the 'Bat Eats Bear' series to be exhibited at a gallery.

DOLLY HAIR-DO'S

① Bette wears pinned braids

② its a Shirley Temple for Lil

③ a ponytail for Trixie.

④ PINCURLS ON PETRA

⑤ Hanna sports a bob

There were big hairy bears
with long claws,

medium hairy bears
with loud roars,

and small hairy bears
with pink paws.

<
Lydia Garner
Dolly Hair Dos
Category Self Promotion
Medium Pencil
Brief I decided to create a self-promotional,
interactive children's book called 'Hello Dolly'.

Sam McCullen
Hairy Bear
Category Children's Books
Medium Mixed media
Brief Hairy Bear set off home with his new friends.
Commissioned by Anne McNeil
Client Hodder Children's Books

Hairy Bear
Category Children's Books
Medium Mixed media
Brief Furlington Village Bear Festival.
Commissioned by Anne McNeil
Client Hodder Children's Books

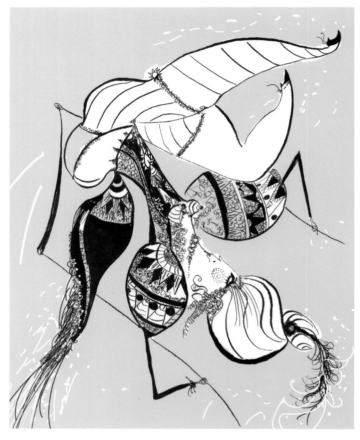

Chichi Parish
Dancer, The Dance And The
Creature With A Back Of Steel
Category Self Promotion
Medium Ink
Brief Self promotion.

How I Feel When I Eat Chocolate
Category Self Promotion
Medium Ink
Brief Mail shot.

>
Lois Bort
Innocence
Category Self Promotion
Medium Charcoal
Brief Experimental work about
how vulnerable children are.

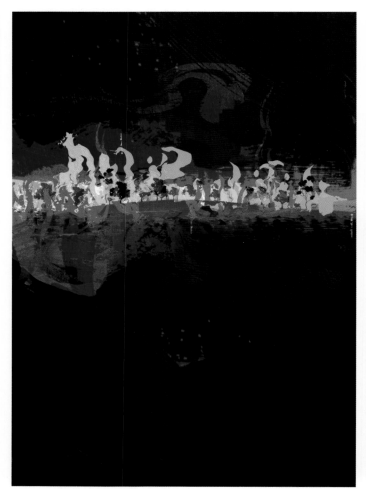

Simon Pemberton
The Songlines By Bruce Chatwin
Category Books
Medium Mixed media
Brief Illustrate the passage "that night.. they watched the rim of the horizon on fire.. the tops of the eucalyptus had been breaking off into fireballs and flying in the gale-force winds".
Commissioned by Sheri Gee
Client Folio Society

Super Volcanoes
Category Editorial
Medium Mixed media
Brief Eruptions of super volcanoes discovered to have been responsible for causing the mass migration of Neolithic peoples.
Commissioned by Craig Mackie
Client New Scientist Cover

>
Lizzie Mary Cullen
Zizzi Italian Restaurants, Covent Garden
Category Design
Medium Acrylic and ink
Brief Zizzi are undergoing a national rebrand in 105+ locations. I'm commissioned to create wall murals in their restaurants that reflect the local area in my style. Themes; Covent Garden theatres and dance.
Commissioned by Nicola Bruce and Holly Paine
Client Zizzi

Grace Alton
Doctor Doctor!
Category Self Promotion
Medium Digital and mixed media
Brief A quirky and humorous illustration
created for promotional purposes.

Ruth Rowland
Aruba Ad Campaign - Girls
Category Advertising
Medium Ink
Brief I was asked to develop a style of lettering and
illustration for each poster that reflects something
of the inhabitants' personalities and interests.
Commissioned by Amy Houston
Client Lowe NY
Commissioned for Aruba Tourism
Photography by Jonas Karlsson

Aruba Ad Campaign - Waitress
Category Advertising
Medium Ink
Brief I was asked to develop a style of lettering and
illustration for each poster that reflects something
of the inhabitants' personalities and interests.
Commissioned by Amy Houston
Client Lowe NY
Commissioned for Aruba Tourism
Photography by Jonas Karlsson

Dorothy
Slieve Donard Hotel
Category Design
Medium Acrylic
Brief The brief was to create a set of individual
paintings of the hotels in the Hastings Hotel Group.
Commissioned by Joanne Harvey
Client Hastings Hotel Group Ltd

Stormont Hotel
Category Design
Medium Acrylic
Brief The brief was to create a set of individual
paintings of the hotels in the Hastings Hotel Group.
Commissioned by Joanne Harvey
Client Hastings Hotel Group Ltd

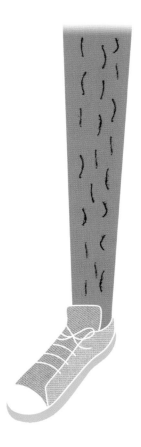

Gemma Robinson
Working Together
Category Self Promotion
Medium Digital and mixed media
Brief Create an illustration on the theme of 'Working Together', specifically alluding to the new coalition government.

Working Together
Category Self Promotion
Medium Digital and mixed media
Brief Create an illustration on the theme of 'Working Together', specifically alluding to the new coalition government. The second in a set.

Phil Wrigglesworth

Gay Pride
Category Advertising
Medium Digital and mixed media
Brief I was asked to create an image aimed
towards Gay Laws by combining Gay Pride
festivals and Lawyers/Law elements, the
image was to be used on promotional material
distributed at Gay Pride Festivals.
Commissioned by Guy Barnett
Client Blakemores Solicitors
Commissioned for Blakemores Solicitors

Grumpy Leaders
Category Editorial
Medium Digital and mixed media
Brief I was asked to illustrate a piece about
grumpy leaders and how many wars have been
started due to lack of sleep.
Commissioned by Bruno Haward
Client The Guardian Weekend Magazine

Sarah Hipsley
Walkabout Planner
Category Design
Medium Digital and mixed media
Brief To illustrate Australian flora and
wildlife and promote tourism to Australia.
Commissioned by Glen Davis
Client Tourism Australia UK

Illustrated Map Of Australia
Category Design
Medium Digital and mixed media
Brief To create a decorative, illustrated map
of Australia depicting Australia's main tourist
areas and icons, as well as visually showing
the locations of places to visit.
Commissioned by Glen Davis
Client Tourism Australia UK

Scott Balmer
The Big Daddy
Category Self Promotion
Medium Digital
Brief This was created to be a part of an exquisite corpse which involved a form of transformation.

The Major's Marvellous Majestic Automobile
Category Self Promotion
Medium Digital
Brief This piece is more of an experimentation. It started life as a pencil drawing and then, using a Wacom tablet, was made into a vector in Illustrator where colour was added to create this retro piece.

From The Far-Out Reaches Of The Galaxy
Category Self Promotion
Medium Digital and mixed media
Brief This one started life as a pencil drawing and was recreated with my Wacom tablet in Illustrator. Once all the elements were complete it was further edited in Photoshop.

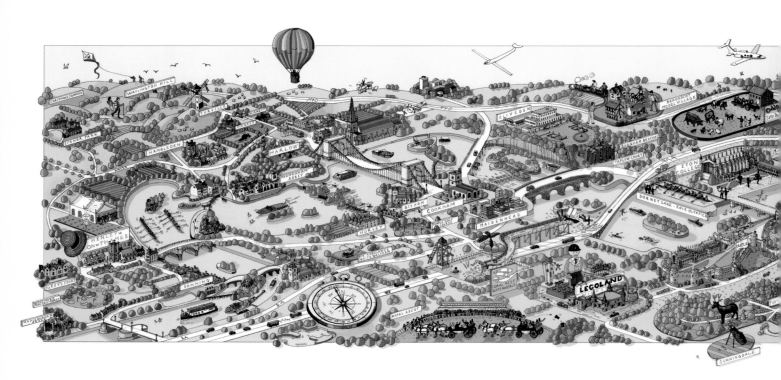

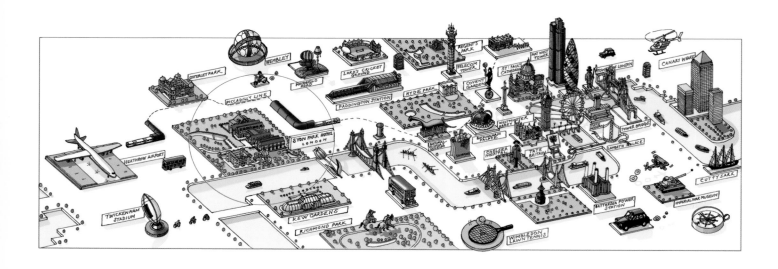

Katherine Baxter
Explore-On-Thames
Category Advertising
Medium Digital and mixed media
Brief To illustrate the River Thames from Henley
to London via Runnymede-on-Thames, for The
Runnymede on Thames Hotel, to be used as an
eight metre mural in the foyer of the Hotel.
Commissioned by Daniel Levy
Client Runnumede on Thames Hotel

London Syon Park Hotel
Category Advertising
Medium Digital and mixed media
Brief To illustrate the location of the new Hilton
Waldorf Astoria Hotel in Syon Park, Brentford.
Commissioned by Scott Roberts
Client February
Commissioned for Hilton Hotel Group

Modern Pentathalon
Category Design
Medium Mixed media
Brief To illustrate the the Olympic modern Pentathalon,
comprising of five disciplines, swimming, shooting,
fencing, running and horse jumping.
Commissioned by David Hillman
Client Studio David Hillman
Commissioned for The Royal Mail

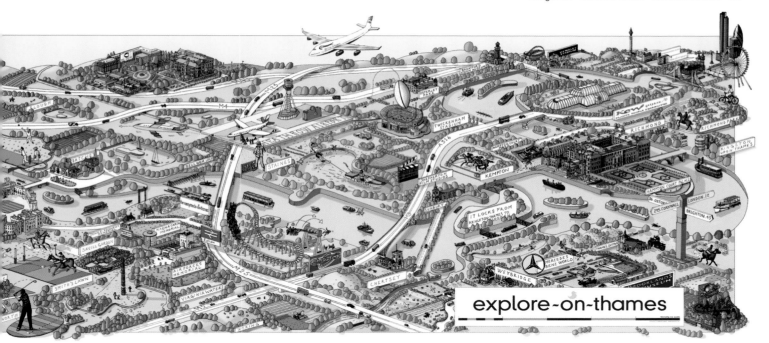

Bee Willey
Mouse Raid
Category Children's Books
Medium Mixed media
Brief The mice about to the raid a
camp of invaders in Egypt.
Commissioned by Carol Katz
Client Tradewind Books

Preeta In The Woods
Category Children's Books
Medium Mixed media
Brief Main character in the Pantchatantra
stories, running through the woods.
Commissioned by Judith Escreet
Client Frances Lincoln

>
Paul Thurlby
A For Awesome
Category Children's Books
Medium Mixed media
Brief To produce an alphabet different from
the many versions around.
Commissioned by Mike Jolley
Client Templar
Commissioned for Paul Thurlby's Alphabet

Ian Whadcock
Power Rangers
Category Editorial
Medium Digital
Brief Big companies with large carbon footprints are to be policed by the Environment Agency from April.
Commissioned by John Poile
Client Director Publications
Commissioned for Director Magazine

A World Of Connections
Category Editorial
Medium Digital
Brief A world of connections. Special report on the state of social media and how social-networking technologies create considerable benefits for the businesses that embrace them, whatever their size.
Commissioned by Una Corrigan
Client The Economist

Fast Track To The Top
Category Editorial
Medium Digital
Brief Doing your job well is a good start. But if entrée to the elusive executive suite is your goal, you have to think strategically.
Commissioned by Gretchen Kirchener
Client Imagine Publishing
Commissioned for PM Network

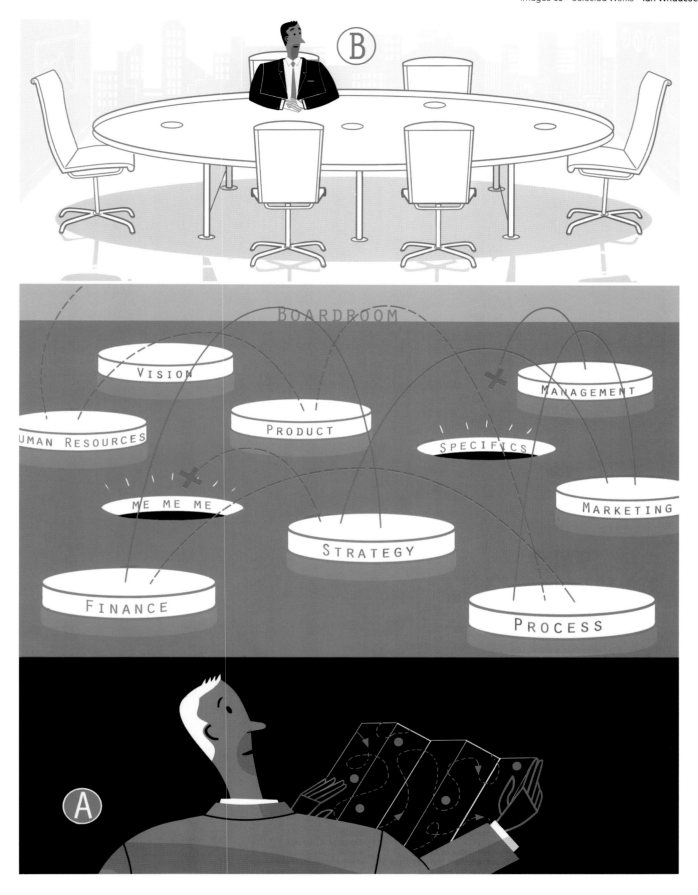

Robin Boyden
Music Marries Money
Category Self Promotion
Medium Digital
Brief File sharing finds a happy union between fans and the music industry through the Spotify music streaming application.

Nuclear Escapism
Category Self Promotion
Medium Digital
Brief Illustration commenting on the 2009 trend in cinema for post apocalyptic, 'end of the world' movies (The Book of Eli, The Road, 2012 etc).

Bipolar
Category Self Promotion
Medium Digital
Brief Illustration exploring the nature of the illness Bipolarity (a form of depression).

Collateral
Category Self Promotion
Medium Digital
Brief More families use home as collateral to secure loans in the wake of financial recession.

Valentina Cavallini
White Rabbit
Category Self Promotion
Medium Collage
Brief To create a set of 12 postcards depicting
characters from classic fairy tales.

Legend Of Paride
Category Self Promotion
Medium Collage
Brief To create an illustration depicting a significant
moment from Laura Orvieto's "Stories of the History
of the World", a children's book of Greek myths.

The Hullaboom
Category Self Promotion
Medium Collage
Brief Inside illustration for children's book. Text:
"Do you think what you saw was a hullaboom?"

Roger Wade
Would It Hurt To Smile Once In A While?
Category Self Promotion
Medium Digital
Brief I've been having nightmares about
Gordon Brown's smile. He looks like he's in
agony, maybe this picture explains why his
smile looks so unnatural.

The Beautiful (Modern) Game
Category Self Promotion
Medium Digital
Brief A picture about how sponsorship and
money has corrupted 'the beautiful game'.

>
Aine Cassidy
Freaky Horoscopes
Category Self Promotion
Medium Digital and mixed media
Brief My personal twist on the signs of the zodiac.

Catherine Brighton
Wooosh!
Category Children's Books
Medium Watercolour
Brief Keep Your Eye on the Kid: The Early Years
of Buster Keaton by Catherine Brighton.
Commissioned by Simon Boughton
Client Roaring Brook Press USA

Steven Carroll
A Man O' Letters
Category Self Promotion
Medium Digital
Brief To create a likeness of poet and lyricist
Robert Burns using only the letters of his name.

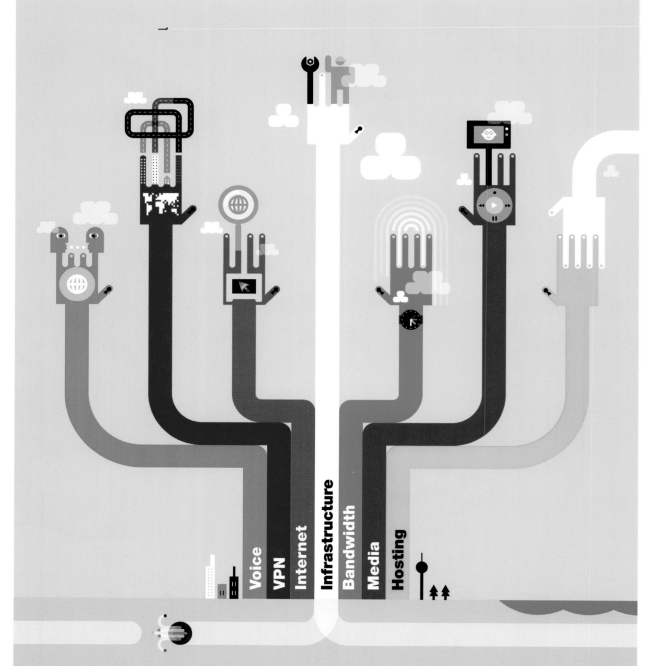

Voice
VPN
Internet
Infrastructure
Bandwidth
Media
Hosting

interoute
from the ground to the cloud

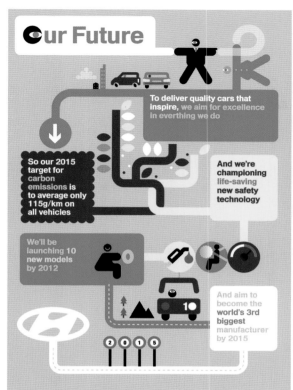

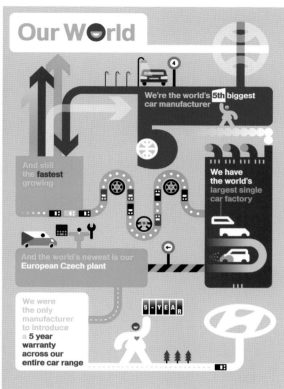

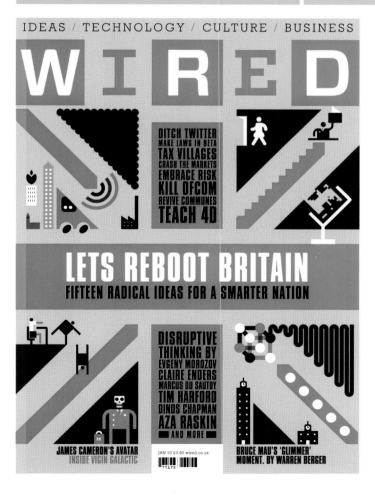

Peter Grundy
Interoute Product Tree
Category Design
Medium Digital
Brief Create a series of iconographic
images to represent Interoutes' various
communication products.
Commissioned by Rebekah Brown
Client Remarkable Things
Commissioned for Interoute

Hyundai Posters
Category Advertising
Medium Digital
Brief A journey to explain the ecological and
economical benefits of Hyundai cars. Told in
a future world and a present world.
Commissioned by Simon Warden
Client M&C Saatchi
Commissioned for Hyundai

Wired
Category Editorial
Medium Digital
Brief Create a cover for 'Let's Reboot Britain'.
Commissioned by Steve Peck
Client Wired UK

Tony Healey
Hendrix
Category Self Promotion
Medium Pencil and digital
Brief One of a set of coasters used to promote the AGM Agency. Each artist represented was asked to produce an iconic image on a 1960s/1970s theme. The set of 40+ coasters was mailed on to clients.
Commissioned by Anna Goodson

Eliot Spitzer
Category Editorial
Medium Ink and digital
Brief Illustration was to accompany a book review "Rough Justice: The Rise and Fall of Eliot Spitzer."
Commissioned by Kristin Lenz
Client The Washington Post

Rafa Nadal
Category Editorial
Medium Pencil and digital
Brief Illustration was used to accompany a profile on Rafael Nadal. A weekly back page profile for the Monday Sport section of The Daily Telegraph.
Commissioned by Wayne Caba
Client Telegraph Group

Ben Steers
Gone Karting
Category Self Promotion
Medium Digital
Brief Series of 12 images for a show entitled "Play" at the East Gallery on Brick Lane, which form part of a narrative surrounding a lonely bear who spends his time playing in his woodland environment.

Moonrise
Category Self Promotion
Medium Digital
Brief Series of 12 images for a show entitled "Play" at the East Gallery on Brick Lane, which form part of a narrative surrounding a lonely bear who spends his time playing in a woodland environment.

Peskimo
Tea Stack
Category Self Promotion
Medium Digital
Brief We wanted to experiment with combining different aspects of work into one image, namely typography and character design. A shelf of tea boxes proved the perfect subject for this.

Jerry Hoare
The Early Bird Catches The Worm
Category Self Promotion
Medium Scraperboard
Brief One of many that I am working on for
a potential illustrated book of proverbs and idioms.

NHS Tree Of Temperance
Category Design
Medium Scraperboard with digital colour
Brief To illustrate the 'Tree of Temperance' but
with the discs announcing elements of NHS care.
Commissioned by Sir Liam Donaldson
Client Twenty Two Design Ltd
Commissioned for Cover for the 2009 Annual report
of the Chief medical officer.

Let The Dog See The Rabbit
Category Self Promotion
Medium Scraperboard, watercolour and digital colour
Brief One of many that I am working on for a
potential illustrated book of proverbs and idioms.

Frazer Hudson
Pig Piano
Category Editorial
Medium Digital
Brief Illustrate Elton John's musical reworking
of the classic dystopian story 'Animal Farm'.
Commissioned by Andrew Mayers
Client The Guardian, Comment and Debate

Cumbrian Dignity
Category Editorial
Medium Digital
Brief Just one week on from the mass
shootings by taxi driver Derrick Bird
in Cumbria depict the local peoples
compassion and dignity in the glare of
the media spot light.
Commissioned by Andrew Mayers
Client The Guardian

Free Mann
Category Editorial
Medium Digital
Brief Depict Simon Mann's recent release from
a 34 year jail sentence in Equatorial Guinea.
Refer to part of the article which describes him
as an 'amphtamine-charged canary'.
Commissioned by Andrew Todd
Client The Guardian

Face Off
Category Editorial
Medium Digital
Brief With one week to go before the general
election 2010 depict the idea of opposition
parties facing each other in the final battles
towards victory.
Commissioned by Sarah Bolesworth
Client The Guardian

Scott Jessop
Liguria Map
Category Editorial
Medium Mixed media
Brief An illustrated map accompanying an article on this culinary rich region of Italy.
Commissioned by David Rice
Client The Sunday Times Travel magazine

Thai Sea Bass
Category Self Promotion
Medium Digital and mixed media
Brief For a range of recipe postcards.

Stuart McReath

Language Opportunities
Category Self Promotion
Medium Mixed media
Brief The benefits and opportunities in learning languages for medical practitioners.

Red Paint
Category Self Promotion
Medium Mixed media
Brief Communism developing into Fascism.

Child Abuse
Category Self Promotion
Medium Mixed media
Brief Child Abuse.

Blue
Category Self Promotion
Medium Mixed media
Brief Sorrow from heartbreak.

Susan Monk
Alexander The Great
Category Self Promotion
Medium Digital and mixed media
Brief Non-commissioned illustration for book cover
- 'Myth & Reality' - Alexander the Great.

Old Nick
Category Self Promotion
Medium Ink
Brief Non-commisioned work for series of
illustrations for children's book of horror stories.

The Vatican Sayings No 34

Ian Pollock
Vatican Saying No 34
Category Self Promotion
Medium Ink and collage
Brief One of 81 illustrations for
"The Vatican Sayings" by Epicurus.

Michael Jackson
Category Editorial
Medium Watercolour, ink and gouache
Brief Full page portrait of Michael Jackson.
Commissioned by Gary Cochran
Client Telegraph Magazine

BICYCLOPS

IGNITING
INNOVATION IN
EDUCATION

Andy Potts
BBC Proms 2010
Category Advertising
Medium Digital
Brief To create the main brand image for the BBC Proms 2010 to promote the music festival across all platforms.
Commissioned by Martin Premm
Client Premm Design
Commissioned for BBC

Bicyclops
Category Self Promotion
Medium Digital
Brief To create an image for a bicycle-centric exhibition called 'Beautiful Machine' at the Howies store in Bristol.

Spark: Igniting Innovation In Education
Category Design
Medium Digital
Brief To create illustrations for a mobile exhibition based on technology in learning.
Commissioned by Ben Carruthers
Client Futurelab

Cycling In London
Category Self Promotion
Medium Digital
Brief To create an image for Transport For London to promote cycling in the capital.

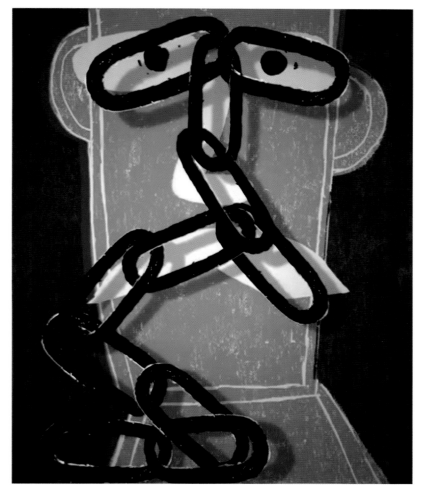

Daniel Pudles
Clive James Isn't A Sceptic, He's A Sucker-But
This May Be The Reason
Category Editorial
Medium Woodcut and digital
Brief George Monbiot on the psychology and
behaviour of climate change deniers over 65.
Commissioned by Roger Browning
Client The Guardian, Comment and Debate

I'd Take Helmand Over Westminster Any Day
Category Editorial
Medium Woodcut and digital
Brief Patrick Hennessey on the launch of his book,
on being a soldier in Afghanistan.
Commissioned by David Gibbons
Client The New Statesman
Commissioned for The Diary page

Crackdown On The Big Green Gathering
Category Self Promotion
Medium Woodcut and digital
Brief To create a short animation based on one of
my Guardian illustrations. The perceived threat of
political activism and its ensuing elimination by
some public authorities.

Peter Ra
Love
Category Books
Medium Digital
Brief Create cover on the theme of love.
Commissioned by Bernard Caleo
Client Cardigan Comics
Commissioned for Tango 9

Doctor Why – Vatikana. Book 1 of 6
Category Self Promotion
Medium Digital
Brief Design a graphic novel about a
supernatural journey through hell.

Anna Alfut
Symbian World Calendar 2010
Category Design
Medium Digital and mixed media
Brief Create scenes from Symbian World (visual environment that supports Symbian brand) to be used as a free desktop wallpaper calendar. Symbian is an open source platform for mobile devices.
Commissioned by Annabel Cooke
Client Symbian Foundation
Commissioned for Symbian Calendar 2010

Alice In Wonderland
Category Self Promotion
Medium Digital and mixed media
Brief Personal work - set of illustrations for Alice's Adventures in Wonderland. Two selected images show King of Hearts and the Footman characters.

<

Andy Robert Davies
Spring Is Sure To Follow.
Category Self Promotion
Medium Digital
Brief This image is part of a series using illustrative
typography to depict quotations about the seasons.

Zara Picken
Photographic Memory
Category Self Promotion
Medium Digital
Brief An illustration from a self-initiated project
combining inanimate objects with figures, in order
to convey aspects of the human condition.

Starman
Category Self Promotion
Medium Digital
Brief An illustration inspired by
the David Bowie song 'Starman'.

Adrian Barclay
If I May...
Category Self Promotion
Medium Digital and mixed media
Brief Produced for illustrated poster exhibition to
the theme 'if I may...'. To use only black and blue
ink. Reproduced as giclée print at A1 size.

If I Was...
Category Self Promotion
Medium Digital and mixed media
Brief Produced for illustrated poster exhibition to
the theme 'if I was...'. To use only black and red.
Reproduced as giclée print at A1 size.

IF I WAS...

CAR
OLD · SIMPLE · FAST · NO CAR · LUXURY · FAMILY · CLASSIC

CHAIR
ERGONOMIC · OPTIMISTIC · AFFABLE · CONCEITED · CONSERVATIVE · ELEGANT · AMIABLE

KITCHEN APPLIANCE
INDUSTRIOUS · MODEST · CONGENIAL · UTILITARIAN · NEGLECTED · GEEKY · ARROGANT

HISTORICAL FIGURE
HENRY VIII · MARIE ANTIONETTE · EINSTEIN · CLEOPATRA · CHAPLIN · MOZART · BLACKBEARD

NUMBER
SMALL · SLOW · LONG · LARGE · LUCKY · PRIME · POSITIVE

INSTRUMENT (MUSICAL)
OBSOLETE · ETHNIC · CONFIDENT · PORTABLE · ELEMETARY · CONVIVIAL · GREGARIOUS

CREATURE
SEA · MYTHICAL · TINY · HAIRY · SPACE · MECHANICAL · PREHISTORIC

HOME
MODERN · STATELY · HOMELESS · HOLIDAY · MOBILE · HUMBLE · NO PLACE LIKE

MISCELLANEOUS
ORGANISED · GLAMOROUS · AMBITIOUS · ROMANTIC · UNDERSTATED · DEFENSIVE · CONTENT

Jill Calder

Hibernacula Woods
Category Self Promotion
Medium Digital and mixed media
Brief Create an animal image that
had atmosphere and wasn't cute.

The Urban Fox
Category Self Promotion
Medium Digital and mixed media
Brief Create a topical animal image
without being cute.

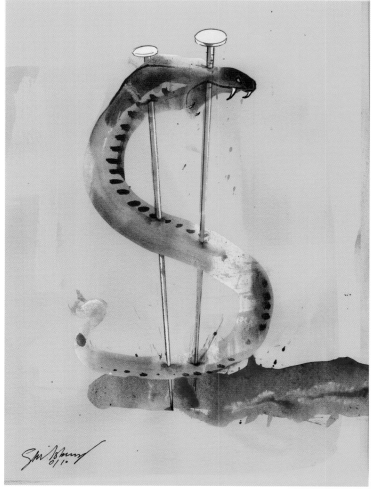

Simon Spilsbury
Guerillanica
Category Self Promotion
Medium Digital and mixed media
Brief To create an image entitled 'If I were...".
Commissioned by Julia Beazley
Client Central Illustration Agency
Commissioned for Annual Calendar

Snakedollar
Category Editorial
Medium Ink
Brief A one-word brief - Money.
Commissioned by Paul Davis
Client The Drawbridge

Builtbypeople Skull
Category Self Promotion
Medium Screenprint
Brief To build imagery with simple figures
that can morph into any shape, anywhere.

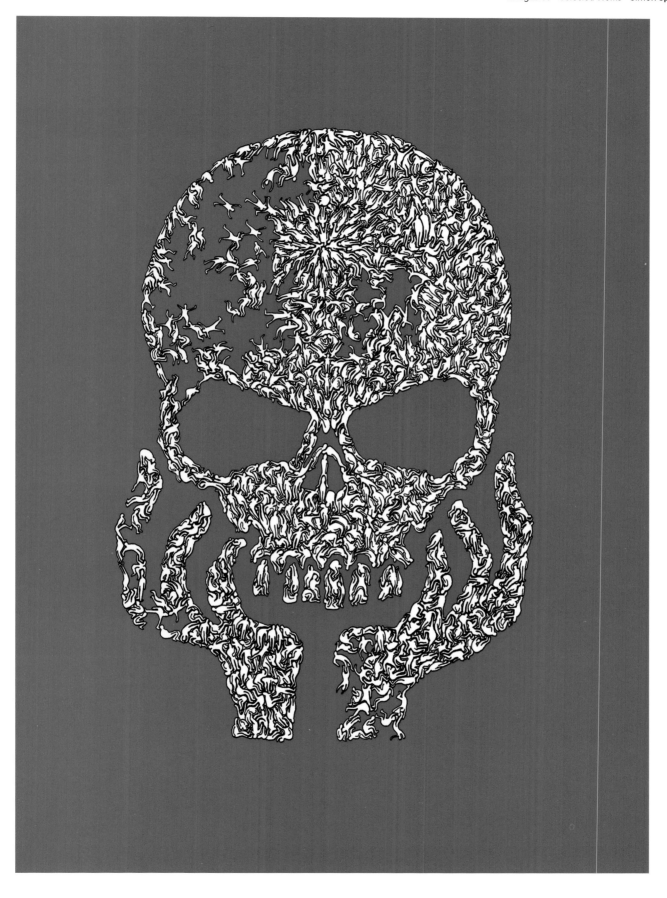

Jasmine Chin
Becoming An Academic
Category Editorial
Medium Digital
Brief To illustrate a case study describing the obstacles and rewards faced on the long journey to PhD success.
Commissioned by Dr Jessica March
Client University of Reading
Commissioned for Oxford Learning website

The Great Switcheroo
Category Self Promotion
Medium Digital
Brief To illustrate Roald Dahl's twisted short story The Great Switcheroo - a moral tale about a man's lustful desire and his comeuppance.

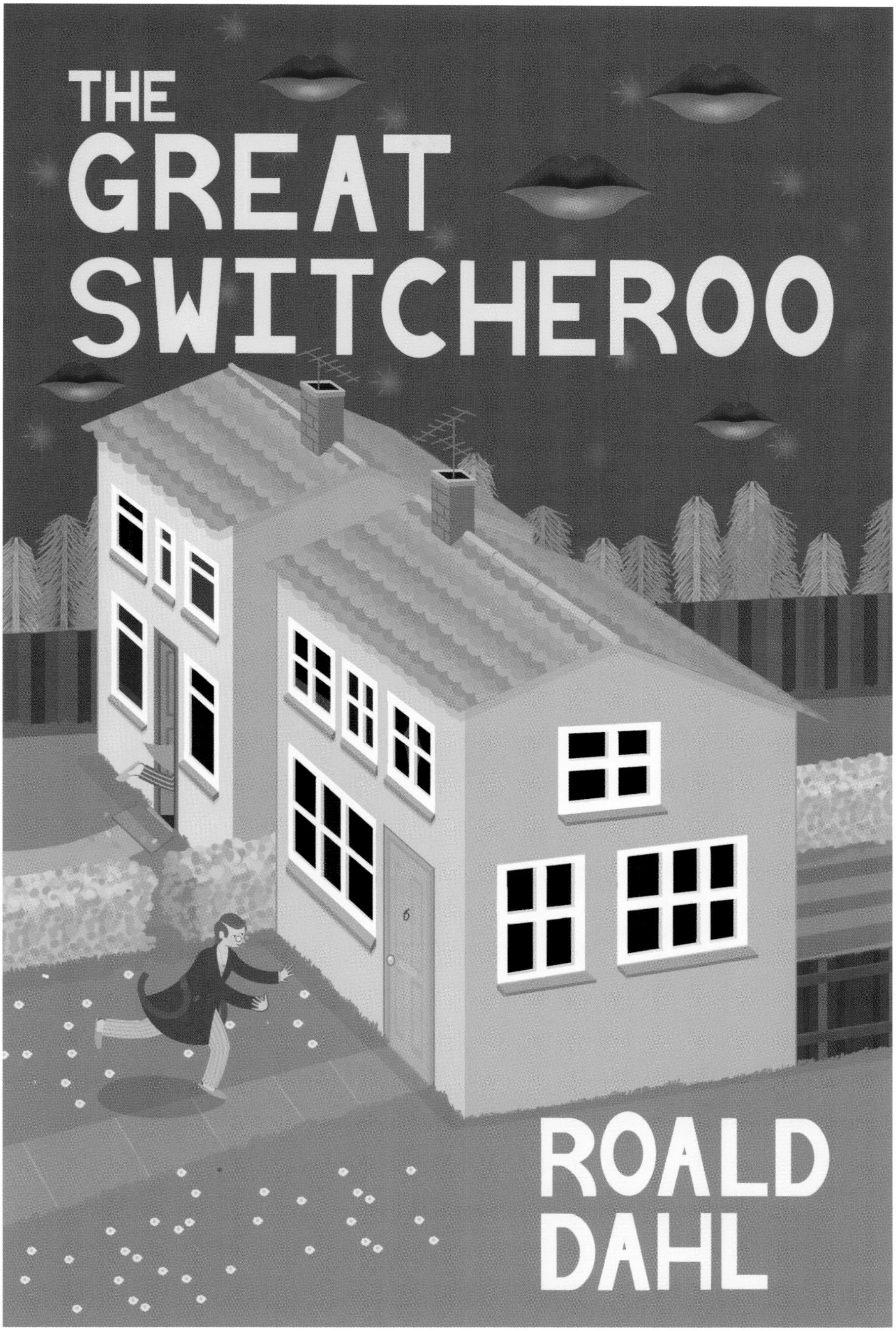
THE GREAT SWITCHEROO
ROALD DAHL

Simon Farr
Thought Crime
Category Editorial
Medium Ink watercolour
Brief Dummy cover illustration about illegal/
immoral/incorrect thinking (unpublished).
Commissioned by Kuchar Swara
Client Swara and Co
Commissioned for The Spectator

NHS Burdon - New Year's Day
Category Editorial
Medium Ink, watercolour and digital
Brief Guardian Comment Cartoon for
new year's day.
Commissioned by Libby Brooks
Client The Guardian

Vic Lee

East London Stories
Category Self Promotion
Medium Screenprint
Brief Creation of dubious stories and amazing facts of East London's full and varied history as a limited edition print.

Kingsland Road E8
Category Self Promotion
Medium Screenprint
Brief The Londonereas series. Limited edition prints of the best places in London to live, eat and shop.

Church Street N16
Category Self Promotion
Medium Screenprint
Brief The Londonereas series. Limited edition prints of the best places in London to live, eat and shop.

KINGSLAND Road

Part of the four boroughs, Dalston, Shacklewell, Newington & Kingsland. So named after the King's Land, once a sprawling wood, the hunting grounds of a Tudor Royal residence where roamed, wild bulls, stags and boars, much as is today. The old Kingsland became Dalston, derived from Derleston which in time was taken from Dedriaf's Tun, the Farm.

This Dalston, home of Dudleys Dept. Store, where fashionistas sought silk Ballito stockings and cramped corsets. The home of the Rio, lest we forget Fairyland, Gaumont, Kings, Gainsboro, the Amhurst and other cinematic gems. This home of penny boutiques and exotic eateries, of skinny jeans, hapless heels and bravado bags. Of the Boosh, disco-balls, underground dancehalls & pouts.

KINGSLAND ROAD

KINGSLAND ROAD

KINGSLAND ROAD

KINGSLAND ROAD

The heart of Dalston - The coolest place in London no less

CHURCH STREET

STOKE NEWINGTON - THE TOWN IN THE WOOD, WHERE LIVES CHURCH STREET ONCE CONNECTED TO CUT THROAT LANE, WHERE ONCE STOOD OPEN FIELDS AND LIVED A VILLAGE AWAY FROM STINKY LONDON TOWN. THE HOME OF THE NOUVEAU RICHE AND MAJESTIC HOMES. WHERE BOHEMIANS, ARTISTS & POLITICAL RADICALS CREATED & BERATED FULL OF NORTHERN PRIDE, LADEN LATTES, BURGUNDY LOAFERS, ORGANIC BANGERS, BUGGIES AND PARK LIFERS SWEEPING STATEMENTS OF UNREQUITED WISDOM TO UNSUSPECTING SOUTHERNERS. WHERE BANKSY BLURRED THE ROYALS TO A CRAZY BEAT.

Stoke Newington

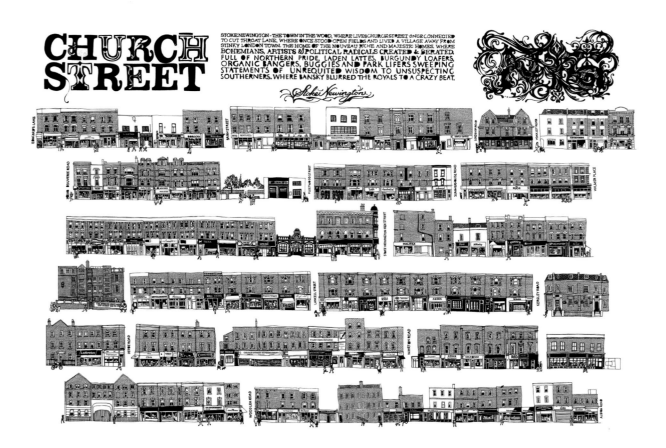

Steve Simpson
Absolut
Category Advertising
Medium Acrylic and ink
Brief To create an original A1 piece of art
that reflected the iconic Absolut brand. The
bottle should be in someway represented in
the image. Otherwise it was completely open.
Commissioned by Bren Byrne
Client The Small Print
Commissioned for Absolut

Lulu And The Noisy Night
Category Books
Medium Digital and mixed media
Brief 32 page Children's picture book
for 2 to 4 year olds. The same palette is
used throughout.
Commissioned by Tadhg Mac Dhonnagáin
Client Futa Fata

Inferno Sauce
Category Design
Medium Digital and mixed media
Brief To design & illustrate a pair of chilli
sauce labels with a gripping brand identity
for a new company. The labels needed to
work as a pair and really stand out from what
was already on the shelf.
Commissioned by Michael Wejchert
Client Mic's Chilli

Catherine Sweetman

B Is For

Category Self Promotion

Medium Ink, collage and digital

Brief To create a more challenging alphabet book.
A broader vocabulary is developed by bombarding
the viewer with a cacophony of images.

Cycling Defining London

Category Self Promotion

Medium Ink, mono print and digital

Brief Create a poster to promote cycling as
innovative, healthy, inclusive and fun way
of getting around London.

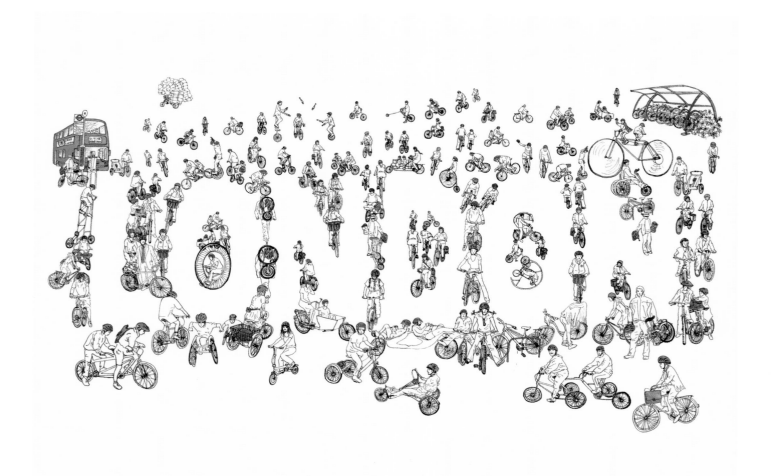

Even in the rain there CAN be a rainbow

Caroline Tomlinson
Pedal Power
Category Self Promotion
Medium Collage
Brief To create an illustration that promotes
the environmental advantages and efficiency of
cycling in London for Transport For London and
AOI competition.

Even After The Rain There Can Be A Rainbow
Category Self Promotion
Medium Collage
Brief To create an illustration that reflects a
more positive view of the recession.

Food Waste
Category Self Promotion
Medium Collage
Brief Highlight the amount of food wasted
with each meal.

Caroline Tomlinson
Don't Throw It Away
Category Advertising
Medium Collage
Brief To illustrate the small changes we
can all make to help the environment.
Commissioned by Shanie Connard
Client CST Advertising

Batteries Not Included
Category Advertising
Medium Collage
Brief To illustrate the small changes we
can all make to help the environment.
Commissioned by Shanie Connard
Client CST Advertising

>
Stuart Briers
Duality
Category Editorial
Medium Digital and mixed media
Brief To illustrate the duality of biomedical
and materials science engineering.
Commissioned by Monica Banaszak
Client Carnegie Mellon

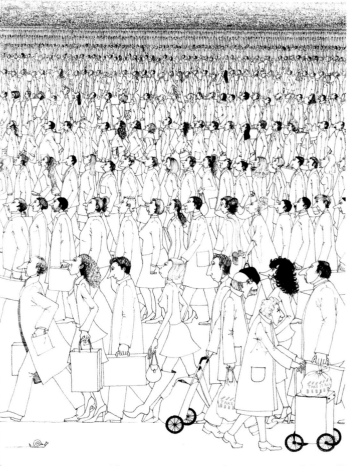

Gwen Turner
Dawn In Darlesville
Category Self Promotion
Medium Watercolour, pen and ink
Brief The cover design for the first episode of
my graphic novel series: Domestic Bliss.

Growth
Category Self Promotion
Medium Watercolour, pen and ink
Brief A full page scene with characters from
my graphic novel series Domestic Bliss.

Commuters
Category Self Promotion
Medium Pen and ink
Brief A page from my graphic novel series
Domestic Bliss.

This Way That Way
Category Self Promotion
Medium Pen and ink
Brief A full page scene from my graphic novel
series Domestic Bliss.

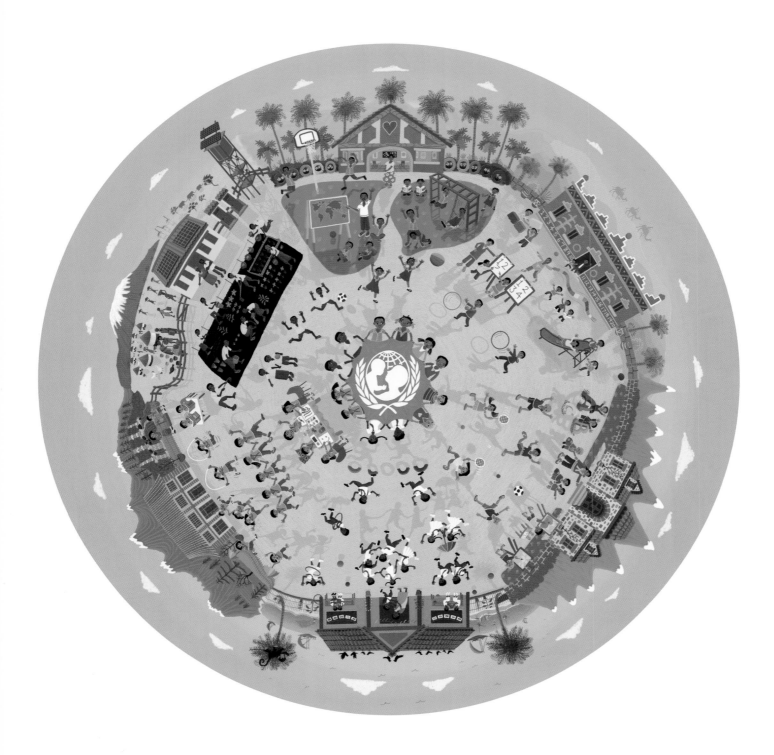

Stephen Waterhouse
Global Playground
Category Design
Medium Digital and mixed media
Brief To create a bright, colourful and positive image showing six schools from different parts of the world in which UNICEF work.
Commissioned by Alice Richard
Client UNICEF
Commissioned for UNICEF Jigsaw

The Small Island
Category Children's Books
Medium Digital and mixed media
Brief To create 35 illustrations for a collection of bedtime stories written by John Goodwin for Lion Children's Books.
Commissioned by Jacqui Crawford and Lois Rock
Client Lion Children's Books

Stephen Waterhouse
Chocolate Production Line
Category Design
Medium Digital and mixed media
Brief To create colourful artwork showing an
imaginary conveyor belt production line depicting
the chocolate manufacturing process. From cocoa
farmers in Ghana through to the final chocolate
hearts which are to be in the calendar.
Commissioned by Tom Mitchell and Kathryn Samson
Client Divine Chocolate Ltd
Commissioned for Chocolate Advent Calendar

Jonathan Williams
Lead Your Pack
Category Editorial
Medium Digital
Brief To illustrate England rugby captain
Steve Borthwick giving a locker room talk to
a range of personalities: the prima donna,
the nervous newcomer, the jaded veteran,
the volcano, the mistake maker...
Commissioned by Donovan Walker
Client Dennis Publishing
Commissioned for Men's Fitness

Jonathan Williams
Keep Walking
Category New Media
Medium Digital
Brief To create a moving pop-up book for the
navigational page of Johnny Walker's Asia website.
'The Pact Among Men' follows the fortunes of four
friends walking the path to greatness.
Commissioned by Michael Chu
Client Ogilvy One Beijing
Commissioned for Diageo

Žižek And Politics
Category Books
Medium Digital
Brief Cover illustration for a critical but appreciative
introduction to the celebrated Lacanian Marxist
and philosopher, Slavoj Žižek.
Commissioned by Lianne Vella
Client Edinburgh University Press

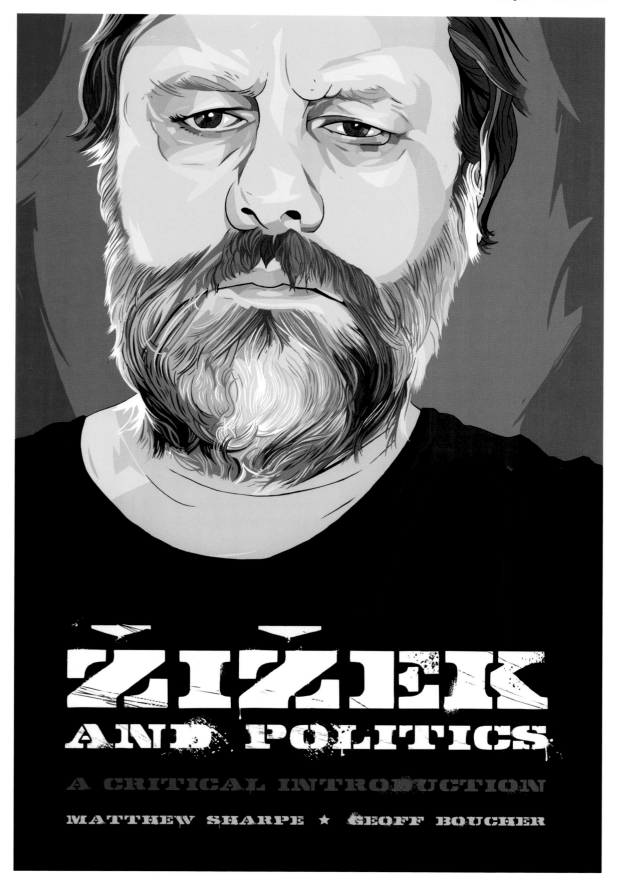

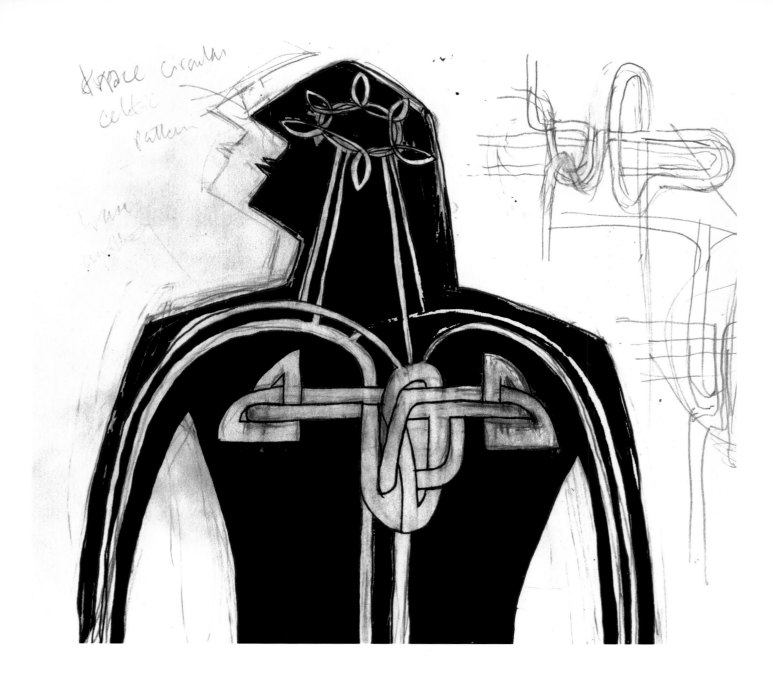

Rhys Bevan Jones
Are You A Celt?
Category Books
Medium Pencil, ink, printmaking and digital
Brief I was asked to illustrate a collection of
poems by leading Welsh bards. This illustration
accompanies the poem Are you a Celt?, and
includes references to anatomy and Celtic patterns.
Commissioned by Gomer Press
Client Gomer Press
Commissioned for Lluniau yn fy mhen
(Pictures in my head)

Simon Brader
The Donor Trail
Category Editorial
Medium Digital and mixed media
Brief To accompany a review of the Radio 4 play
'The Donor Trail' - an emotional journey of a donor
heart told from both sides of the affected families.
Commissioned by Ped Millichamp
Client BBC
Commissioned for Radio Times

Bright with a beauty that is not its own

TELL

NO 1

Jackie Parsons
In Pursuit Of Beauty
Category Editorial
Medium Mixed media
Brief Open brief to provide a full page
opening image for a Chapter of the
publication entitled "In Pursuit of Beauty".
Commissioned by Matt Roden
Client .Cent Magazine

Untitled
Category Self Promotion
Medium Mixed media
Brief One of 4 images
produced for promotional book
to be published Spring 2011.

Paul McBride
Tony Benn In Conversation
Category Self Promotion
Medium Digital and mixed media
Brief A self initiated illustration of a talk
I attended at the Bloomsbury Theatre.

Phil Wheeler
State Of Nature
Category Self Promotion
Medium Digital and mixed media
Brief The online 7 Sins Contest asked for my take
on the seven deadly sins. Living in a state of
nature, these pink beings just can't stop sinning,
despite all the natural abundance.

Pascale Carrington
The Fish Supper
Category Self Promotion
Medium Digital and mixed media
Brief To produce an image of the foods
we eat, and our relationship with them.

Black Coffee Project
Fear
Category Editorial
Medium Digital and mixed media
Brief To illustrate "Fear". Show
someone in the grip of fear and create
the heading of the article to work on a
double page spread.
Commissioned by Pauline Doyle
Client The Guardian Weekend

Cyberwar: The Threat From The Internet
Category Editorial
Medium Digital and mixed media
Brief Show how the future of warfare
is changing from the battlefield to the
microchip, and how the push of a button
can bring a country to its knees.
Commissioned by Penny Garrett
Client The Economist

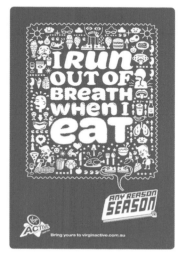

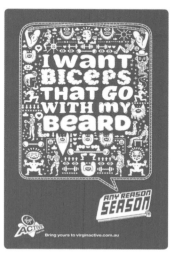

Serge Seidlitz
Sinalco's Swiss Summer
Category Advertising
Medium Digital
Brief A map of Switzerland as an island with all the summers activities it offers.
Commissioned by Andrea Bachofner
Client Rod Kommunication
Commissioned for Sinalco

Any Reason Season
Category Advertising
Medium Digital
Brief Campaign based on the reasons people have to go to the Gym - any reason will do.
Commissioned by Alison Dunlop
Client Publicis Mojo
Commissioned for Virgin Active gyms

Andrew Foster
Southbank Centre
Category Design
Medium Mixed media
Brief To capture the energy and mood of the
new classical season at the Southbank Centre.
Commissioned by Peter Silk & Rob Steer
Client Silk Pearce

>
Paul Wearing
Quality
Category Design
Medium Digital
Brief For the company EOS's 2011 calendar,
illustration to convey the concepts of Visions,
Looking ahead, Thinking about it, Solution
orientated, Stability of Value. Unpublished.
Commissioned by Sylvi Egert
Client The Ad Store
Commissioned for EOS Calendar

Butterfly
Category Self Promotion
Medium Digital
Brief Limited Edition Print.

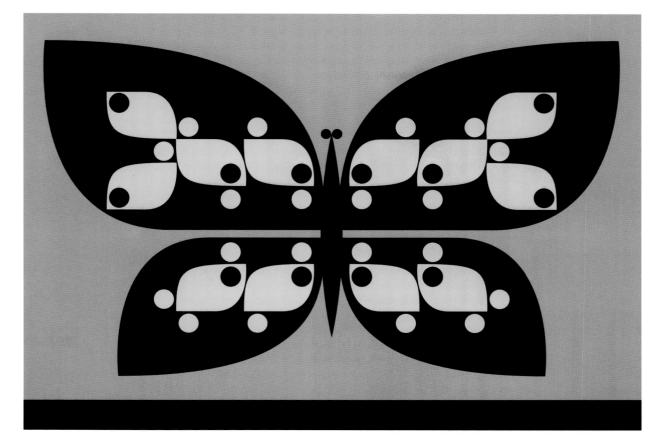

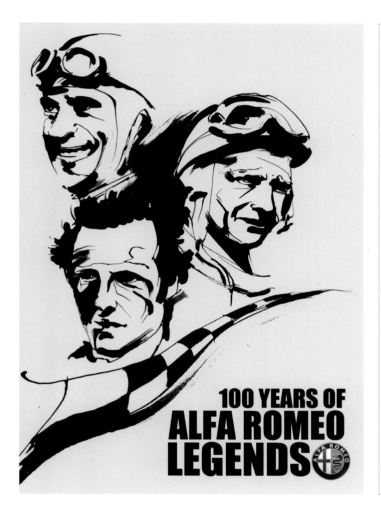

<

Antony Cattini
Little Monsters
Category Self Promotion
Medium Digital and mixed media
Brief An illustration depicting two infant monsters
playing hide and seek amongst the skyscapers of London.
The illustration was created by overlaying redrawn
photographic images onto watercolour in Photoshop.

Eri Griffin
100 Years Of Alfa Romeo Legends
Category Design
Medium Ink
Brief Illustration is for Official Alfa Romeo Art
Print and events.
Commissioned by Pascal Johanssen
Client Illustrative

Alfa Romeo - One Hundred Years Of History
Category Design
Medium Ink
Brief Illustration is for Alfa Romeo Official Art
Print and events.
Commissioned by Pascal Johanssen
Client Illustrative

Alexis Goodwin
Madge Giving The Scarf To James
Category Children's Books
Medium Digital and mixed media
Brief To illustrate the story of La Sylphide a ballet by
August Bournonville. The book was produced by
The Royal Danish Ballet to introduce young children
to the story of La Sylphide.
Commissioned by Erik Jacobsen
Client Det Kongelige Teater

Chris Garbutt
Bubble Trouble
Category Self Promotion
Medium Digital and mixed media
Brief To create a striking poster image
to showcase the artist's creativity for a
Leeds University Alumni exhibition.

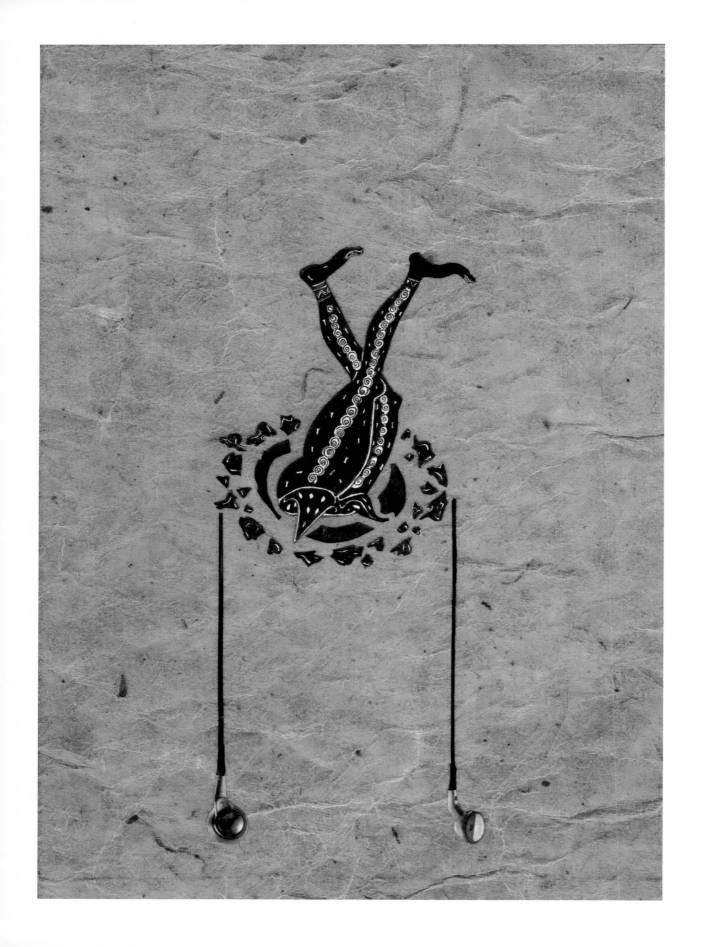

Holly Sims
Information Nation
Category Editorial
Medium Digital and mixed media
Brief Illustration for an article about how landlords are increasingly using social networking tools such as Twitter and Facebook to communicate with their tenants.
Client Ocean Media Group
Commissioned for Inside Housing Magazine

<
Merlin Evans
Pied Piper Trips
Category Self Promotion
Medium Mixed media
Brief Self promotion, a retelling of the Pied Piper of Hamlin tale set in the age of the iPod.

<

Chris Haughton
Stairway To Heaven
Category Design
Medium Digital and mixed media
Brief 5x3 metre mural for the Gibson Hotel in Dublin.
Commissioned by Tim Bebbington
Client Neworld
Commissioned for Gibson Hotel, Dublin

Ian Henderson
The Soldier's Tale
Category Self Promotion
Medium Ink
Brief The first from a set of drawings for the musical drama The Soldier's Tale by Stravinsky and Ramuz.

Bird In The Hand
Category Self Promotion
Medium Gouache
Brief One of a series of stylised graphic works, influenced by Middle Eastern design and colour.

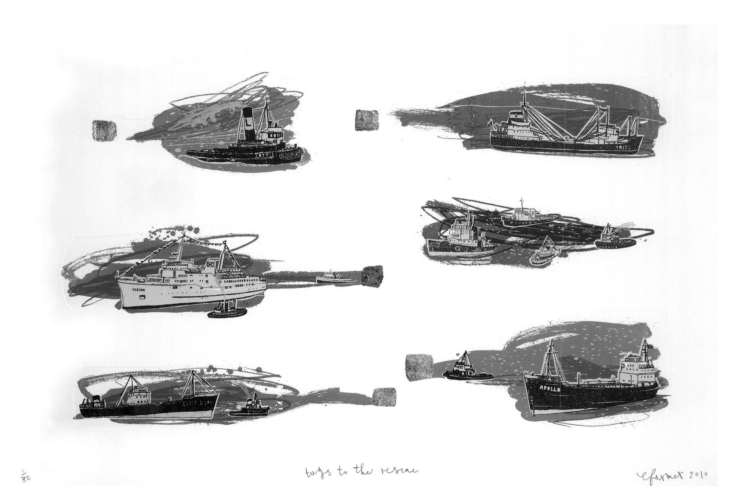

tugs to the rescue

1/30

cfarmer 2010

Charlotte Farmer
Tugs To The Rescue
Category Self Promotion
Medium Screen print with embossed
bottles and gold leaf corks
Brief Personal experiment to combine
embossing and screenprinting.

John Barrett
The King
Category Self Promotion
Medium Ink
Brief Self commissioned artwork produced
as part of a collection of images interpreting
'Poet in New York' by Federico Garcia Lorca.

Matthew Richardson
Spoken Ink (Halloween)
Category Advertising
Medium Digital and mixed media
Brief Create images for posters to advertise
storytelling events by 'Spoken Ink' in the Royal
Parks at Halloween, Christmas and Valentines
Day. This character was used with a different
head for each event.
Commissioned by Charles Chambers
Client Cha Cha Design
Commissioned for The Royal Parks/Spoken Ink

Joe Wilson
The Thousand Autumns Of Jacob De Zoet
Category Books
Medium Ink and digital
Brief Create a rich illustrated book jacket.
Incorporate a sense of drama with simple colour
palette, hinting at the Japanese setting. Needs
a sense of period, and to subtly reflect the love
story within.
Commissioned by Alasdair Oliver
Client Hodder and Stoughton
Commissioned for Hodder and Stoughton/Sceptre

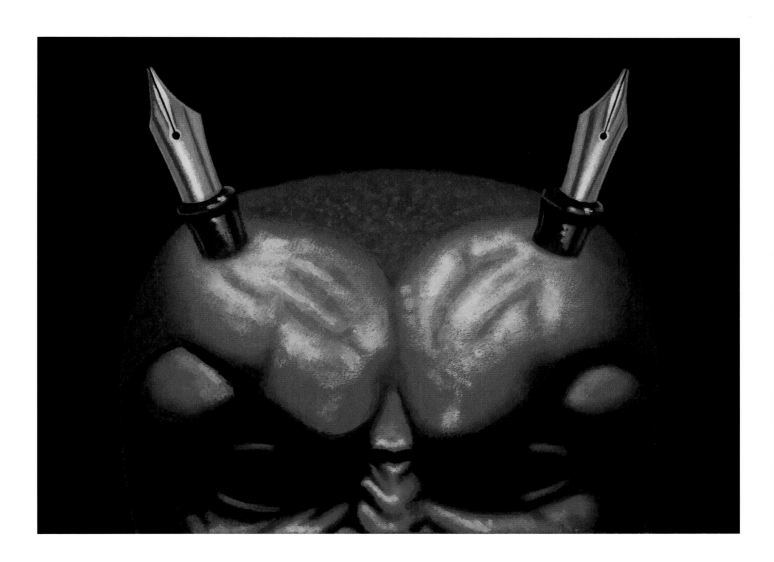

James Fryer
The Turkey That Voted For Christmas
Category Editorial
Medium Acrylic
Brief Higher fees could be the undoing of
England's universities. In voting for higher student
fees, the Russell Group are being likened to
turkeys who vote for Christmas.
Commissioned by Chris Barber
Client TSL Education Ltd
Commissioned for Times Higher Education

Sponsorship
Category Editorial
Medium Acrylic
Brief Giving sponsors power is dangerous and
undermines our trust. Allowing interested parties
to control research publication is wrong.
Commissioned by Chris Barber
Client TSL Education Ltd
Commissioned for Times Higher Education

Poison Pen
Category Editorial
Medium Acrylic
Brief Academic book reviewing has become
negative and irresponsible and can seriously
damage one's career in a time of intense
academic competition.
Commissioned by Chris Barber
Client TSL Education
Commissioned for Times Higher Education

Andrew Gibson
Felixstowe
Category Self Promotion
Medium Digital and mixed media
Brief Observations of Felixstowe.

Katrina Page
The Day The Saucers Came
Category Self Promotion
Medium Digital and mixed media
Brief For a poem by Neil Gaiman, "That day, the
saucers landed...You didn't notice any of this
because you were sitting in your room...just looking
at your telephone, wondering if I was going to call."

Kate Slater
I Dreamt I Was A Whale
Category Self Promotion
Medium Collage
Brief To illustrate one line from the poem
'Dreamer' by Brian Moses.

>
Martin Hyde
The Greyhound
Category Design
Medium Digital
Brief Swinging sign illustration and design forming
the brand identity for the Greyhound Public House
in Derby. The illustration and typography was used
in many guises throughout the venue.
Commissioned by Paul Harris
Client The Real Pub Company
Commissioned for The Greyhound Public House

Rupert Van Wyk
The Empire State Building
Category Self Promotion
Medium Digital
Brief To represent the movement, hustle
and bustle of New York traffic around
the iconic Empire State Building.

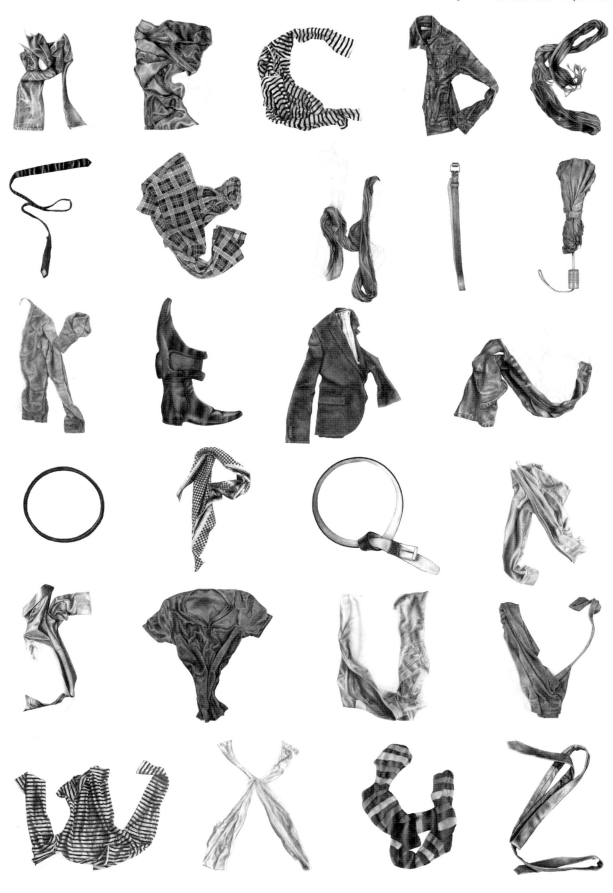

Stuart Whitton
Alphabet
Category Self Promotion
Medium Pencil
Brief A self initiated project
to develop and produce an
alternative approach towards
hand created letters, in order
for the concept to reach
it's full potential the entire
alphabet was illustrated.

Marc Gooderham
Lonely Stretch
Category Self Promotion
Medium Acrylic
Brief One of a series of paintings concentrating
on some of London's decaying and unique
architecture. 61 x 76 cm.

Sam Peet
The Horned One
Category Self Promotion
Medium Digital and mixed media
Brief The idea behind this self-initiated project was
to create a fantastical body of work relating to gods
and mythical creatures from various cultures.

Patrick Hat
The Boss
Category Self Promotion
Medium Digital and mixed media
Brief To illustrate the theme 'the bully in the workplace'.

Tadashi Ura
Sakura
Category Self Promotion
Medium Mainly Ink
Brief The elegant expression through Japanese ink.

Angel
Category Self Promotion
Medium Mainly Ink
Brief The elegant expression through Japanese ink.

〈

Naomi Tipping
GAD
Category Self Promotion
Medium Digital and mixed media
Brief To illustrate the condition
Generalised Anxiety Disorder, an
anxiety disorder characterised by
excessive, uncontrollable worry.

Mark Long
Twitter
Category Self Promotion
Medium Ink
Brief The illustration is about one of my pet hates.
People who are obsessed with updating their
Twitter/Facebook etc at all times. So much so, that
they aren't even enjoying the moment they are in.

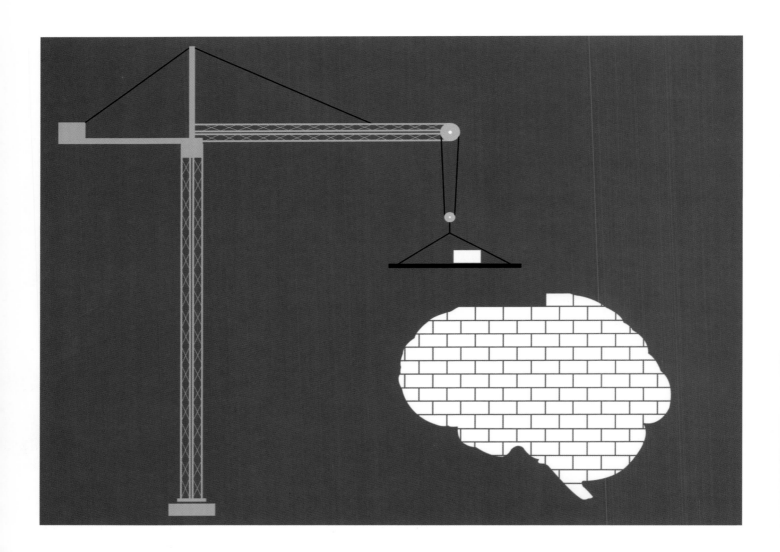

Thomas Phillips
Building Intelligence
Category Self Promotion
Medium Digital
Brief To produce work relating to the
theme 'building intelligence' showing how
my work fits into an editorial context before
contacting construction publications.

>
Dan Stafford
Polyamory
Category Editorial
Medium Digital
Brief Refer to the pride and strength of
conviction held by the polyamory community
to illustrate the complex and colourful nature
of multi-partner relationships.
Commissioned by Edwin Reinerie
Client Winq Media

Jonathan Burton
Janus
Category Editorial
Medium Pencil and digital
Brief The end of the UK Film Council which was the intermediary from government funding to the UK film industry.
Commissioned by Chris Brawn
Client British Film Institute
Commissioned for Sight and Sound Magazine

Heroes
Category Editorial
Medium Pencil and digital
Brief A world where investment bankers are the heroes protecting customers money from a double dip recession.
Commissioned by Mark Stammers
Client Moneywise Publishing
Commissioned for Moneywise Magazine

>
Hannah Thomson
Calming The Storm
Category Self Promotion
Medium Acrylic ink with pencil crayon
Brief Produce a series of paintings for the story, 'Jesus Calms The Storm'. The use of colour is important as is the way that you personify the natural environment to narrate the key parts of the story.

Mark Smith
Annuities: Angels Or Devils?
Category Editorial
Medium Digital and mixed media
Brief The pros and cons of annuities.
Commissioned by Robin Henriquez
Client Source Media
Commissioned for Employee Benefit News

Jan Bowman
Early October Morning, Venice Beach
Category Self Promotion
Medium Digital
Brief Sketched on holiday in LA. 9am, solitary
surfers in black wetsuits, black crows, the sound
of crashing waves, huge sky and that beach hut.

Moseley Artists' Market
Category Self Promotion
Medium Digital
Brief Submission for local art
competition on theme of "Moseley
in Motion". It won first prize.

Kevin Hauff
Factory Flower
Category Self Promotion
Medium Acrylic, collage and digital
Brief Image exploring a general
change in practice where certain
forward thinking manufacturers are
starting environmentally friendly
manufacturing techniques to
replace old polluting methods.

Matthew Cook
Election 2010 Interview: Nick Clegg
Category Editorial
Medium Acrylic inks and collage
Brief Sketch and indicate the surroundings of
The Times Editor and Political Editor interviewing
Nick Clegg on a train to Southampton.
Commissioned by Jon Hill
Client The Times

Election 2010 Interview: Gordon Brown
Category Editorial
Medium Acrylic inks
Brief To sketch The Times Editor and Political
Editor interviewing Gordon Brown whilst
touring Warwickshire College. Three hours to
complete the drawing.
Commissioned by Jon Hill
Client The Times

Russell Cobb
Brainstorm
Category Self Promotion
Medium Ink
Brief To produce a exciting visual essay of imagination, designs, inventions and ideas into a random narrative story.

Gabriel Garcia Marquez

Of Love
and Other Demons

Fatime Szaszi
Of Love And Other Demons
Category Self Promotion
Medium Mixed media
Brief To create a book cover for
"Of Love and Other Demons"
by Gabriel Garcia Marquez.

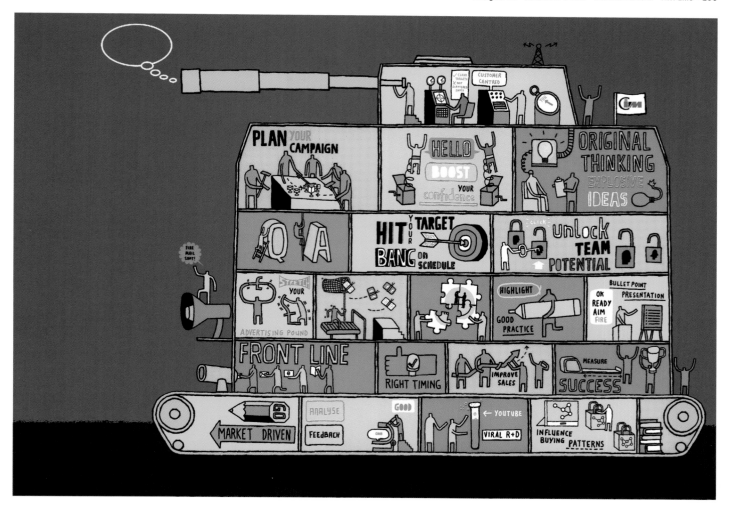

Tim Ellis
Think Tank
Category Editorial
Medium Digital and mixed media
Brief To illustrate theme of Marketing
Communications as a battlefield in
which 'Original Thought' is highly desired.
Commissioned by Karen Fowler
Client White Gate Design
Commissioned for
Chartered Institute of Marketing

Cowboy Builder
Category Editorial
Medium Digital and mixed media
Brief Article on perception of builders in
Yellow Pages and the notion they might
be cowboys.
Commissioned by Mark Bergin
Client Atom Publishing
Commissioned for Construction Manager

David Hughes
The Lord Will Deliver Us.....
Category Books
Medium Pen, ink, watercolour and computer
Brief Provide 13 illustrations for the classic novel
Count Belisarius by Robert Graves, set in the
Roman Empire, 6th century. Here Belisarius is in
self imposed exile praying for guidance.
Commissioned by Sheri Gee
Client Folio Society

10 Days Grace: Senate
Category Books
Medium Pen, ink, watercolour and computer
Brief One of 13 illustrations for the classic novel
Count Belisarius by Robert Graves, set in the
Roman Empire, 6th century: Read the book and
select passages to illustrate.
Commissioned by Sheri Gee
Client Folio Society

Jonathan Gibbs
Eel
Category Books
Medium Wood engraving
Brief To show water, flowing elements of growth
and nature and decay, and the swimming eel.
Commissioned by Miriam Rosenbloom
Client Faber & Faber

Dart
Category Books
Medium Wood engraving
Brief To make an image to complement the poem
Dart, by Alice Oswald, including aspects of the river,
landscape, natural history and the elements.
Commissioned by Miriam Rosenbloom
Client Faber & Faber

Come In
Category Books
Medium Wood engraving
Brief To choose 20 poems, from a collection
of 187, and illustrate them. These are spaced
throughout the book, with additional cover and
spine illustrations.
Commissioned by Sheri Gee
Client Folio Society

Tea Table
Category Design
Medium Wood engraving
Brief To picture a kitchen with a heart.
Commissioned by Charlotte Dean
Client Charlotte's Cot Blankets

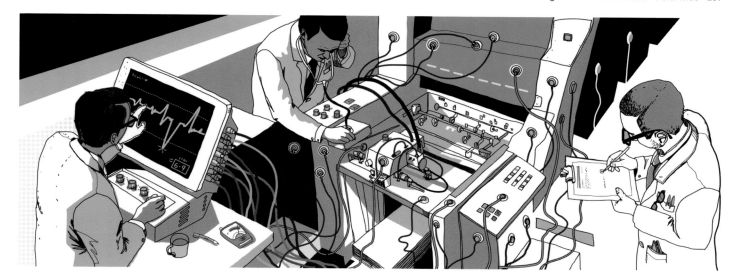

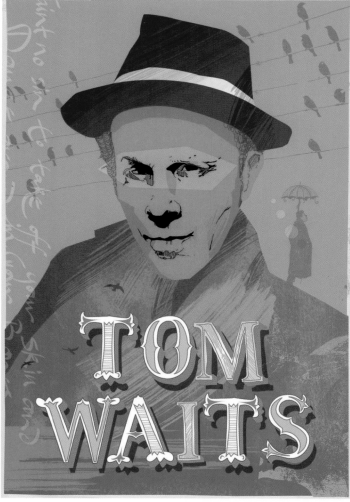

Peter Mac
Event Awards
Category Design
Medium Digital and mixed media
Brief Illustration for The Event Magazine awards cover image.
Commissioned by Kevin Hilton
Client Haymarket
Commissioned for Event Magazine

Health Of The Print Industry
Category Editorial
Medium Digital and mixed media
Brief To illustrate and article about the health of the print industry in the UK today.
Commissioned by Dinah Lone
Client Haymarket
Commissioned for PrintWeek

Tom Waits
Category Self Promotion
Medium Digital and mixed media
Brief I like tom waits and I wanted to capture his soul.

Bin Your Gum
Category Advertising
Medium Digital and mixed media
Brief To advertise the fines imposed by the government for throwing chewing gum on the floor.
Commissioned by Scott Franklin
Client Brey Leino
Commissioned for Chewing Gum Group

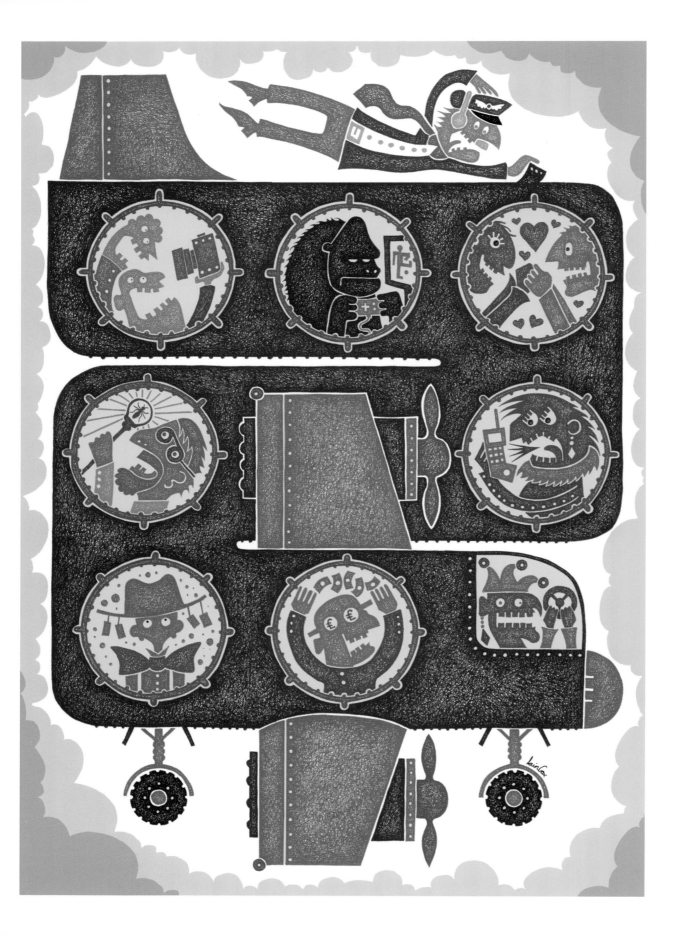

<

Iain Cox
Tales On A Plane
Category Self Promotion
Medium Hand drawn, digitally coloured
Brief Promotional illustration displaying
an eclectic range of stereotypes you may
encounter while flying through the air. Featured
in the Cheltenham Illustration awards.

David Gibson
Fingers Crossed
Category Self Promotion
Medium Digital
Brief Promotional postcard for wide range of
potential clients and competition entries. Published
in The Drawbridge: Money issue.

Tom Jennings
Dashwood
Category Design
Medium Digital
Brief To produce a panoramic drawing of London
to be displayed in the foyer of the Dashwood
building in London.
Commissioned by 300million
Client Land Securities

Escapist
Category Self Promotion
Medium Ink
Brief Personal work.

Two Sides
Category Design
Medium Ink
Brief 6 illustrations for a company concerned with
the promotion of sustainable paper manufacture.
The images were created with natural media to
highlight the tactile nature of paper.
Commissioned by 300million
Client Two Sides

When it comes to paper,
some people can't see
the **wood for the trees.**

If you've been told that paper making destroys
forests, then think again. In Europe, where 94%
of the paper we use comes from, the area
of forest cover is actually increasing by an area
four times the size of London every year.

Print and Paper is probably the most widely
used commodity product made from a natural
resource and is both renewable and recyclable.

Print and Paper is also a powerful way to
communicate with 56% of media buyers
in a recent survey preferring paper based
communications for greater impact.

Renewable, Recyclable and Powerful.

Print and Paper
have a great
environmental
story **to tell**

TWO SIDES

www.twosides.info

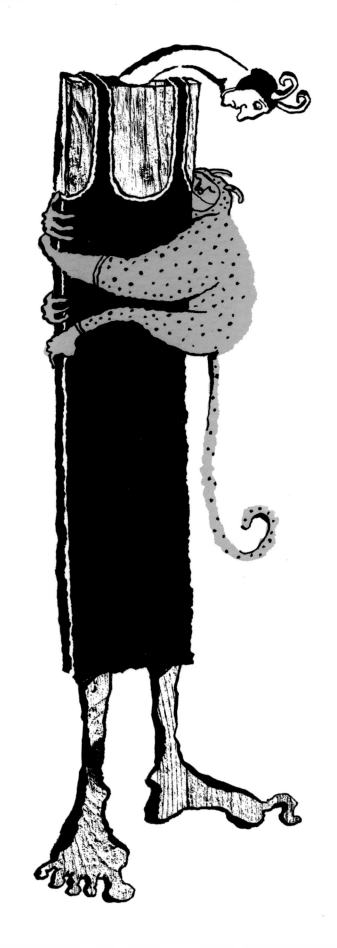

Belle Mellor
Too Tense
Category Self Promotion
Medium Ink
Brief A spread from a melancholy and humorous book about a an inward looking man trapped in his own anxiety. He eventually becomes able to appreciate the world around him.

Infinite Gloom
Category Self Promotion
Medium Ink
Brief A spread from a melancholy and humorous book about a an inward looking man trapped in his own anxiety. He eventually becomes able to appreciate the world around him.

Summer Reading
Category Editorial
Medium Ink
Brief A review of summer reading.
Commissioned by Paul Oldman
Client Smith
Commissioned for Cambridge Alumni Magazine

Laura Meredith
M Is For Meat
Category Self Promotion
Medium Mixed media
Brief One of a series of images based on the theme of culinary deaths. When completed the images will be incorporated into a book which I hope to self publish.

Wendy Plovmand
Laneige: Mystic Veil
Category Design
Medium Digital and mixed media
Brief Create a design with a mystic, feminine, seducing, fairy tale like atmosphere with references to nature and snow crystals. Design is used as an entire piece but details should also work individually.
Commissioned by Anastasia Lee
Client laneige
Commissioned for B&F International Corp

Stroem Coat Of Arms
Category Design
Medium Digital and mixed media
Brief Create an identity design for a unisex fashion store. Design should incorporate elements from female and male universes and manifest itself as both masculine and feminine in terms of shape and color.
Commissioned by Karina Laugesen
Client Stroem

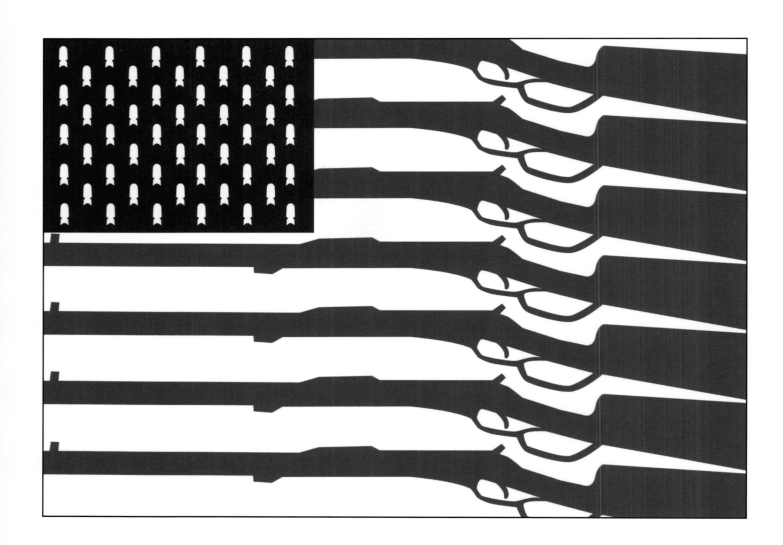

Shuning Qian
Flag Of Pride
Category Self Promotion
Medium Digital
Brief This work is inspired by my
personal opinion against Iraq war.

>
David Rooney
Plutarch Lives
Category Books
Medium Scraperboard
Brief To produce 30 portrait illustrations plus
binding cameos for a 4 vol. set of Plutarch's
biographies of famous Greeks and Romans
written at the beginning of the 2nd century AD.
Commissioned by Joe Whitlock Blundell
Client The Folio Society

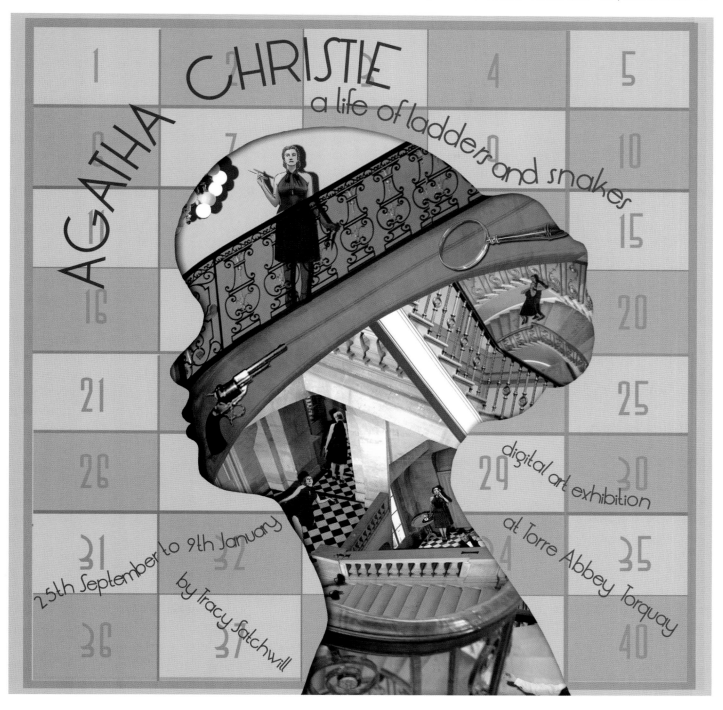

Andrew Baker
Exercise Your Imagination
Category Editorial
Medium Digital
Brief Can a daily saunter through the city do more than stretch the legs? Produced to illustrate a feature by Alexei Sayle for the Guardian's post Christmas dinner edition of the Walk Yourself Fit Guide.
Commissioned by Jeremy Marshall
Client The Guardian
Commissioned for Walk Yourself Fit

Tracy Louise Satchwill
Agatha Christie, A Life Of Ladders And Snakes
Category Self Promotion
Medium Digital and mixed media
Brief I designed a poster to publicise a digital exhibition on the ups and downs of Agatha Christie's life. The exhibition was entitled Agatha Christie, a life of ladders and snakes.

David Sparshott
Manchester City v Birmingham
Category Editorial
Medium Pencil
Brief A weekly illustrated
match report from a Premier
League football match for the
2010/11 season.
Commissioned by Jon Hill
Client The Times 'The Game'

Arsenal v Birmingham
Category Editorial
Medium Pencil
Brief A weekly illustrated
match report from a Premier
League football match for the
2010/11 season.
Commissioned by Jon Hill
Client The Times 'The Game'

Nancy Tolford
Burn Out
Category Editorial
Medium Digital
Brief A woman who is bored with her
sexual relationship with her husband and is
considering embarking on an affair, wants to
know if desire wanes over time in even the
most passionate of relationships.
Commissioned by Martin Harrison
Client News International
Commissioned for The Saturday Times

Valley Of The Dolls
Category Self Promotion
Medium Digital
Brief To accompany a review of this cult classic
novel for a literary blog: illuminatedpage.net.

Tobias Hickey
Work Stalker
Category Editorial
Medium Digital and mixed media
Brief TV producer started receiving abusive e-mails
and calls on an almost daily basis which had a
devastating effect on her confidence and career.
Commissioned by Helen Morrish
Client Mail on Sunday
Commissioned for You Magazine

>

Michelle Thompson
My Love
Category Self Promotion
Medium Screenprint
Brief Development of a
collage called Red Love.

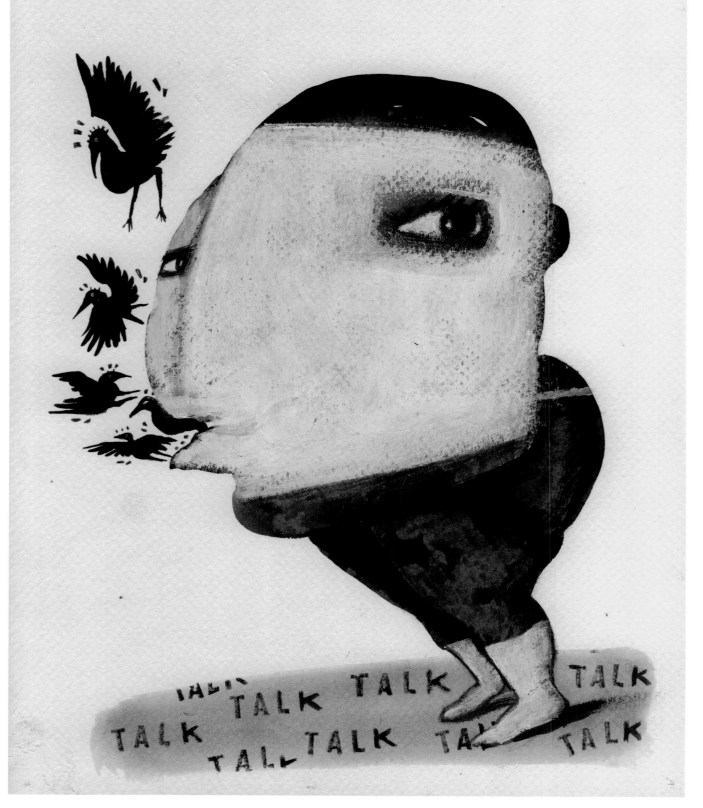

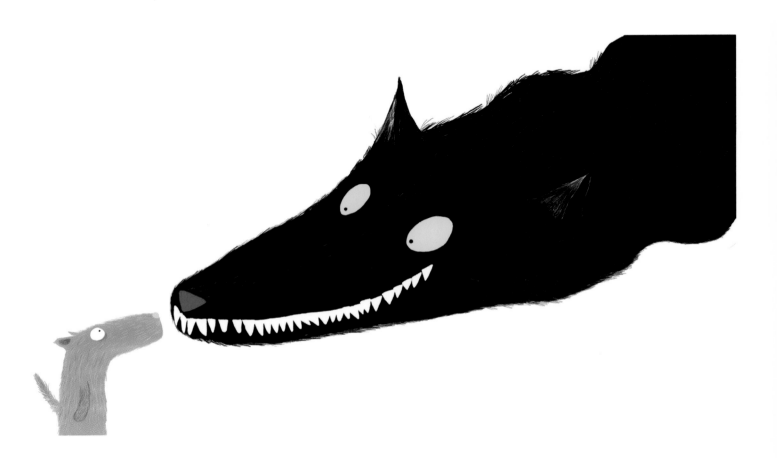

Nadia Shireen
Spread From 'Good Little Wolf'
Category Children's Books
Medium Digital and mixed media
Brief I developed 'Good Little Wolf' during
my MA in Children's Book Illustration at
Anglia Ruskin University. It was published
in June 2011 by Jonathan Cape.
Commissioned by Helen Mackenzie-Smith
Client Random House

<
Jean-Christian Knaff
Talk Talk
Category Self Promotion
Medium Mixed media
Brief Self -promotional image to
show how I feel at this very moment.

<

Portia Rosenberg
The Slaughter Of Cornelius De Witt
Category Books
Medium Pencil
Brief Inside illustration for 'The Black Tulip' by Alexandre
Dumas: the slaughter of Cornelius and Johann de Witt.
Commissioned by Sheri Gee
Client The Folio Society

Neil Stevens
Animation Portfolio
Category Self Promotion
Medium Digital
Brief To create a new homepage illustration that
helped promote the addition of a new section of
the website that showcased animation work.

Ellie Phillips
The Octopus
Category Self Promotion
Medium Ink
Brief To create intricate illustrations of animals
and birds, using patterns as inspiration.

>
Patrick O'Leary
Tree Hugging
Category Self Promotion
Medium Digital and mixed media
Brief Create an illustration that depicts the role
that trees have played in the development of
humanity; in the discovery of fire, gravity, books
and as an elementary building material.

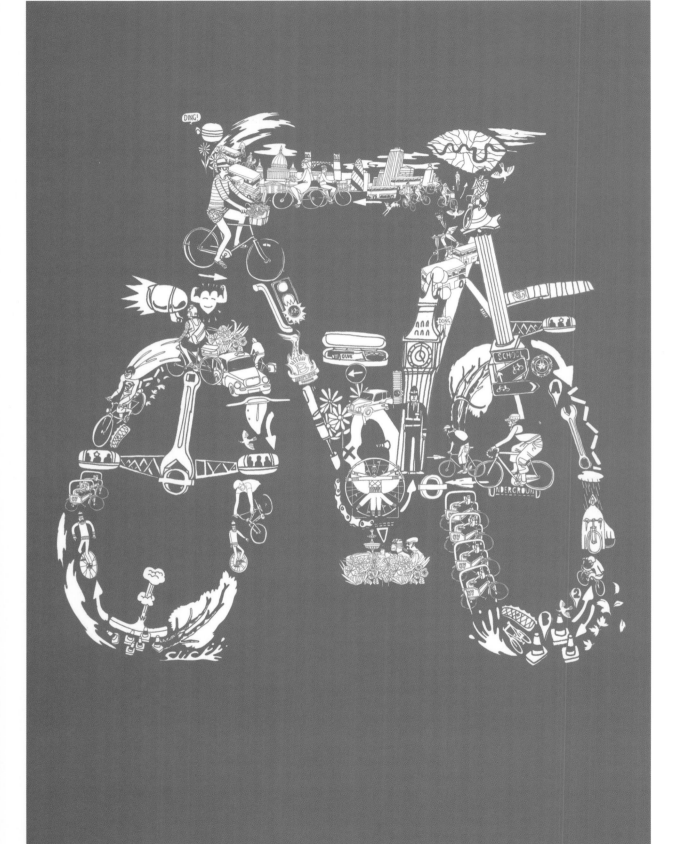

<

Mark Taplin
Bike
Category Self Promotion
Medium Digital and mixed media
Brief Design a poster for London Transport
Museum/AOI Cycling in London competition.
Illustrate the benefits and fun of cycling
in London and promote their new bicycle
share system and new cycle lanes.

Gwendi Klisa
A Visit To The Barbican
Category Self Promotion
Medium Screenprint
Brief My vision of the Barbican.
Created to complement an editorial
about Europe's largest multi-arts venue.

Jinwoo Kim
Cinderella
Category Children's Books
Medium Watercolour
Brief Cinderella story.

Barbara Ana Gomez
Natural
Category Design
Medium Ink
Brief Natural will be printed in black on a cream
fabric and assembled by hand using natural wood
without varnish. The illustration will be beautiful
and original; a nature scene with a surrealist touch.
Commissioned by Sergio Fernandez Gallardo
Client Fancy A Fan

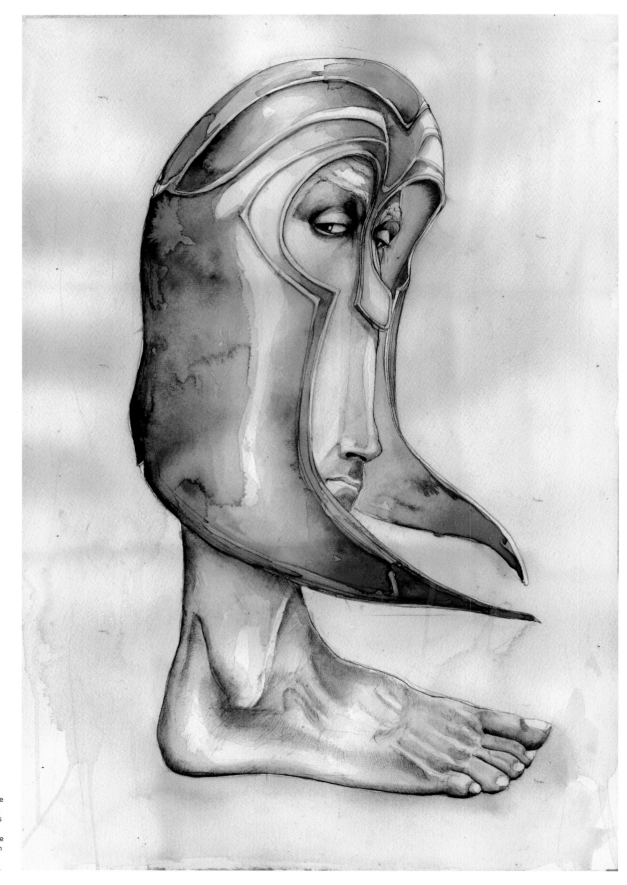

Daniel Mackie
Achilles
Category Self Promotion
Medium Watercolour
Brief Achilles Heel. From the
Greek myth. Achilles was a
great warrior. When he was
a baby his mother dipped
him in the river Styx to make
him immortal. She held him
by his heel which became
his only point of weakness.

Al Heighton
Dining Out
Category Self Promotion
Medium Screenprint
Brief After producing an image for a college catering course I produced this illustration about dining out experience based on fine chefs using and prepping fine produce etc.

‹
Bill McConkey
Kaleidoscope
Category Self Promotion
Medium Digital
Brief To create an eye catching cover for
a self promotional booklet which collects
together visual influences, images from my
childhood and generally things I like to draw.

Masako Kubo
We Are All Big Losers
Category Editorial
Medium Digital and mixed media
Brief To illustrate Oliver Burkeman's
column about why your friends seem
so much more popular than you are.
Commissioned by Bruno Haward
Client The Guardian

Donna Shrestha
A Cloud Of Bats
Category Self Promotion
Medium Lino print and digital media
Brief This illustration is to be part of an
illustrated book of collective nouns.

Teresa Murfin
Naughty Toes
Category Children's Books
Medium: Mixed media
Brief To illustrate the text by Ann Bonwill about a less than graceful little girl trying to master the graceful art of ballet.
Commissioned by Molly Dallas
Commissioned for Oxford University Press

Miriam Latimer
Ruby's School Walk
Category Children's Books
Medium Acrylic
Brief To Illustrate the children's book text: 'Ruby's
School Walk' by Kathryn White. A book about a
girl's fears as she takes her first walk to school.
Commissioned by Tessa Strickland
Client Barefoot Books

〉
EB Hu
Gau Town
Category Self Promotion
Medium Digital and mixed media
Brief Gau Town is EB Hu's up-
coming graphic novel loosely based on
Chinese myth - "Journey to the West".

Lucy Roscoe
Alice
Category Self Promotion
Medium Paper cut
Brief An illustration for Alice's adventures in Wonderland offering a contemporary paper fantasy where shadows show darker undertones of adventure.

>
Steve May
Boy Zero Wannabe Hero
Category Children's Books
Medium Digital
Brief To provide illustrations for the cover and inside of the book about the accident prone wannabe hero and the petrifying plot of the plummeting pants.
Commissioned by Mandy Norman and Lucie Ewin
Commissioned for Faber and Faber

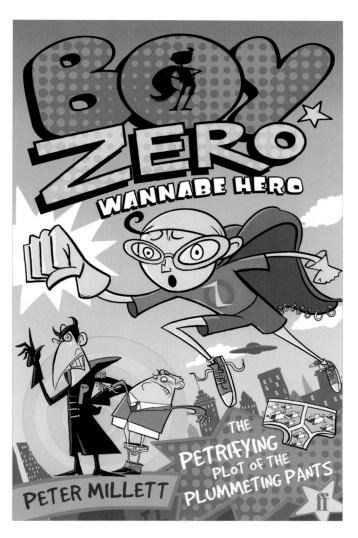

Stephen Collins
Exit Music
Category Books
Medium Ink and digital colouring
Brief Part of a six-page short story for
UK comics anthology.
Commissioned by Tom Humberstone
Client Solipsistic Pop

How To Eat Bugs
Category Editorial
Medium Acrylic and ink
Brief Article about how to survive in the
wild for British Army magazine.
Commissioned by John Butterworth
Client Haymarket
Commissioned for Camouflage Magazine

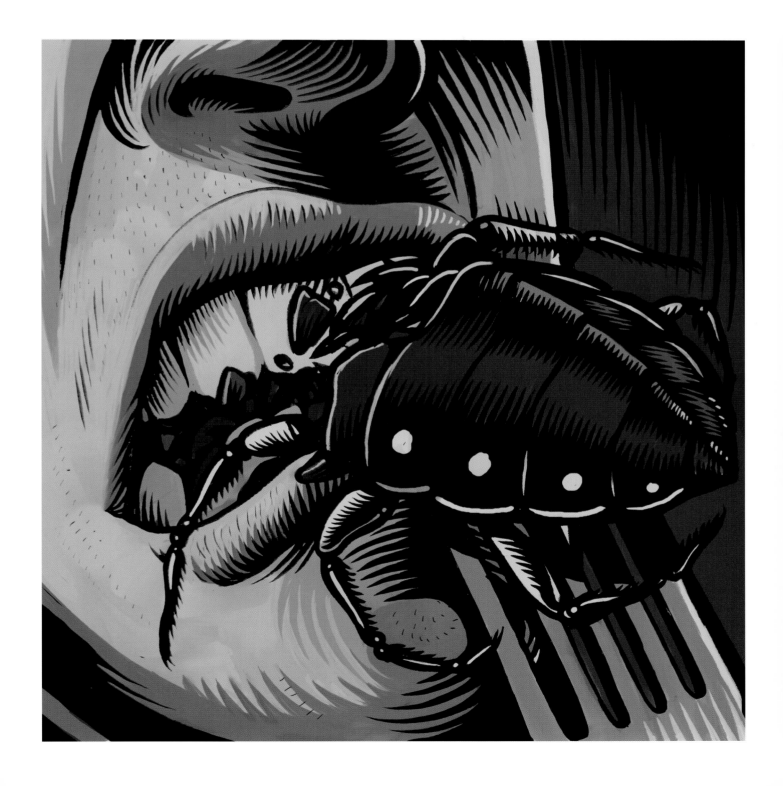

Jonathan Lam
The River
Category Self Promotion
Medium Digital and mixed media
Brief A promotional piece for a
graphic novel titled 'North of the River'.

Harriet Love
It's Dark In Here
Category Self Promotion
Medium Collage, digital and monoprint
Brief From the book series entitled 'Pages from
an Unfolding mind'. The books were inspired by
a child's first visual connection to the world with
the beginnings of verbal communication.

Michael Sheehy
Time And Tide
Category Self Promotion
Medium Mixed media
Brief Transience :The passage of Time,
The River of Life.

Katie Longshaw-Pye
Animal Amputees
Category Self Promotion
Medium Screenprint
Brief I use comical alternatives to the
regular limbs of various animals using
metaphorically similar objects such as
helicopter propellers on a hummingbird
(because you never see their fast wings) etc.

Animal Amputees

Sarah Hanson
Summer In The City
Category Editorial
Medium Digital and mixed media
Brief Illustrate a feature about a persons
bike journey across London showing the
possible places worth a visit along the way.
Commissioned by Sue Herdman
Client National Trust Magazine

^
Tim Marrs
KFC Mural
Category Design
Medium Digital and mixed media
Brief To create a large mural for KFC international. To be used in new and existing restaurants with a "youthful lifestyle" feel.
Commissioned by Bill Leissring
Client Subzero Design
Commissioned for KFC Europe

‹

Glen McBeth
Mummy Medicine
Category Editorial
Medium Pen, ink and digital
Brief Apparently, up until Victorian times, they used ground up Egyptian mummies in an assortment of medicines for an assortment of ailments.
Commissioned by Susanne Frank
Client BBC History Magazine

Darren Diss
Happy Radio
Category Editorial
Medium Mixed media
Brief Illustrate an editorial article that discusses some of the reasons why listening to the radio is such a pleasure.
Commissioned by Dan Barber
Client The Independent

Bad Apple
Category Editorial
Medium Mixed media
Brief Illustrate an editorial article that discusses the way violent killers are influenced by the actions of people around them.
Commissioned by Dan Barber
Client The Independent

Frank Love
Galway Oyster Festival
Category Advertising
Medium Digital and mixed media
Brief A series of three images portraying
interesting events based upon a particular
month - September. Galway's Oyster Festival.
Commissioned by Andrea Plummer
Client Eastwing

Mariachi
Category Advertising
Medium Digital and mixed media
Brief A series of three images portraying
interesting events based upon a particular
month - September. Mexico's Mariachi Festival.
Commissioned by Andrea Plummer
Client Eastwing

Jonathan Penn
The Girl With Balloons In Her Eyes
Category Self Promotion
Medium Pencil and digital media
Brief A character design for a short
animated film about a girl who falls so in
love with a toy balloon that they become
inseparable from one another.

New Talent • Essay
Gary Powell • Designer and Senior Lecturer

Gary Powell has worked as an illustrator/designer/printmaker and educator since graduating from Saint Martins School of Art & Design. Powell has established a significant national and international reputation working on numerous projects that span across editorial, design, advertising, multimedia, including major commissions such as selection for Royal Mail Millennium Stamp Collection; 48 top image makers of Great Britain that included David Hockney, Eduardo Paolozzi, Bridget Riley, Ralph Steadman, Lord Snowden. He has won numerous awards and nominations including D&AD 'Yellow Pencil' silver awards, Asian awards for Illustration, B&H Gold Pencil award. Powell's work has appeared in various publications.

Gary Powell is Senior Lecturer at University of Brighton and MA Communication Design at Central Saint Martins (University of the Arts). Powell has exhibited and spoken at various conferences and Institutions, both national and international, about his work and research activities. His recent research activities include a series of collaborative projects working with community groups (e.g. homeless families). Recently Powell was selected for a project 'Politics into Print', commissioned to respond to government archives as a starting point to translate into images and a series of prints. Another area of his research is on the perceptions of the word 'Black'.

Somebody with a natural or exceptional ability, a gift, an aptitude, flair, capacity, faculty, an endowment, forte, or pure genius, 'talent' can be difficult to quantify. Are you born talented, is it a gift, is talent nurtured, cultivated in good soil? Does it need to be spotted, recognized by others and set apart, that which already sets one apart?

Sometimes we can recognize, identify, or in retrospect trace back those destined for great things, the 'diamond in the rough'. The phrase clearly a metaphor for the original unpolished state of diamond gemstones, especially those despite appearances, that have the potential to become high quality jewels.

Edward de Bono commented that to be successful you have to be lucky, or a little mad, or very talented, or find yourself in a rapid growth field. With the expansion of illustration, the nature versus nurture debate concerns the relative importance of an individual's innate qualities versus personal experiences in determining behavioural traits, abilities and differences. Coached by her father, a

cartoonist who drew images to make her tennis more fun, Monica Seles former no 1 professional tennis player commented 'People think I must have been so talented at an early age, but I don't know - was it talent or hard work? Who knows?'.

For the new generation of illustrators ability and knowledge is of little value if you do not put it into practice and practice. Talent is just the starting point, some will need to work hard to make the cut or be as hard to cut as a rough diamond. Jet Li the Chinese martial arts champion and international film star said, 'I knew nothing about martial arts. The coach told me I was talented, and put me in a school. Three years later I got my first championship in China'.

Students on three-year courses, with talent, need talent to nurture it, encourage and guide it, not just to spot it. One person's talent is another person's... although the selection was not my own; these 'rough diamonds' reflect an international diversity of abilities and sensibilities, content and aesthetics and represent over 20 different places of learning, from around the country.

'In teaching others we teach ourselves.' I remember as a student about to study post-graduate Illustration, with the intention of being under the tuition of an illustrator whose work I greatly admired. Having applied, navigated through a selection process, a place assured, I would now be Luke Skywalker to his Obi-Wan Kenobi. Circumstance, however meant he departed the College the summer before I arrived. I was gutted, but grateful others played their part in challenging, shaping my ideology, working methods and ways of thinking. From the innovative working methods of Mirinae Chang, searching for invisible forms utilizing carbon paper laid on streets as starting point, to others utilising traditional processes such as Adam Cruft etchings documentations and Golbano Moghaddas poetic emotional images about love, the journey of a feminine spirit, are intriguing. From Oliver Butcher observations of swimmers to Martha Zmpounou work inspired by the Jungian 'Shadow' archetype, as part of the unconscious mind, creates

BLKpnthr by Jerome Miller
Burst by Martha Zmpounou
Laugh Your Head Off by Perter Gamlen
Rainbowcoalition by Jerome Miller
Red, White & Black by Paul Layzell
Seed (fantasy biology series) by Katie Scott
Monster Idea 3 Smile by Pat Bradbury

images that explore our hidden weaknesses and repressed instincts. Visually appealing, layered with hidden meaning. My mind reflects on other bright talents outside of this book. Jerome Miller's sophisticated Black Panther images, reveals a highly skilled draughtsman and graphic sensibilities. Katie Scott's biological/botanical images have time-honoured appeal with a refreshing contemporary edge. The humour of Peter Gamlen's 'Laugh your head off', Paul Layzell comic visuality in 'red, white and black' or Pat Bradbury multidisciplinary graphic crossover images, which have an updated 1980's feel. My talent list could go on.... And so could yours.

I always thought it would be better to be a fake somebody than a real nobody. (Tom Ripley in the film The Talented Mr. Ripley). As a society we are obsessed with programs that profess to spot talent (Pop Idol, X Factor, Fame Academy, Britain's got talent etc) Susan Boyle's image belied a talent now appreciated by a much wider audience. In illustration terms talent is out there, those trying to find their voice, wanting the chance to show potential, to find an audience. It can be easy to delight in the efforts of others, or as perceived talent is unmasked, revealed as unsubstantiated. Those with greatest potential for growth laughed at. Albert Einstein was certain he had no special talent; curiosity, obsession and dogged endurance, combined with self-criticism, brought him to his ideas, he claims.

Unfortunately many hope for more visual intelligence and creativity than they are prepared to work towards, some less obsessive than they should be, maintaining aspirations without perspiration, expecting dividends without investment. Regurgitating things without irony. Surfing the Internet, picking up on visual style that can devalue work, in danger of wanting instantaneous success. Placing work on the Internet when not fully formed, not yet tried and tested. Before students have found their voice, some are stars of the blogs, being profiled, giving a false impression of success, misleading profile of work, a misconception of the level of ability and potential of the creator.

JF Kennedy once said all of us do not have equal talents, but all of us should have an equal opportunity to develop our talents. As an educator, developing and challenging your talented students is just as important as nurturing those with less natural ability, who with hard work have the potential to be just as talented.

There are great Institutions to study, but some seats of learning have become 'bums on seat', students as customers; consumers; commodities, the commercialisation of learning continues. Lack of talent rewarded for commercial gain, rigorous academic judgment sidelined on the economic playing field. With major educational changes ahead will students benefit, get what they pay for, or pay for what they do not get?

Even with increased student numbers, illustration should be more than a dot-by-dot or paint-by numbers activity. Connect the dots, is a form of puzzle (a problem, enigma or brief that tests the ingenuity of the solver) containing a sequence of numbered dots with hidden things to discover. For some students Illustration is the subject that joins up the dots between many aspects of their life and sensibilities, their curiosities, areas of interests, observations and interpretations; emotions, content and aesthetics, word and image etc whilst for others it is more of a dot to dot activity, to replicate what someone else has pre determined. In adult discourse the phrase 'connect the dots' is used as a metaphor to illustrate an ability to associate ideas, to find the 'big picture', or salient feature, in a mass data and cognitive development.

Talented people can accomplish great things, but everyone needs someone in their corner, Muhammad Ali had Angelo Dundee. 'I could have been a contender', when talent is not taken to its defining moments or opportunities, potential remains just that, potential. Illustrators, understand your practise, the creative community. It is our responsibility to encourage, nurture and utilize new talent to elevate it and our profession to greater heights.

New Talent Refresh! Award • Gold

Sponsored by The Coningsby Gallery

Rob Hodgson
They Shot Him Down

College University of Plymouth
Medium Pencils, crayons and computer
Brief Myth making as an image maker.
Course BA Hons Illustration
Course leader Ashley Potter

Rob Hodgson was born in Torquay where he spent his summers cleaning swimming pools and listening to a lot of sad sack music.

He moved to Plymouth to study illustration at university.

Rob has a basic interest in mark making and representation, and a deep interest in how pictures affect myth and memory. Ultimately he likes good drawings.

He also loves to write and most of Rob's work is based around or directly related to narrative.

Some inspirations are: early 20th century European painters, 40's fiction writers, 50's illustration, 60's pop music, nature, space, truth, big and small things, adventures and cavemen.

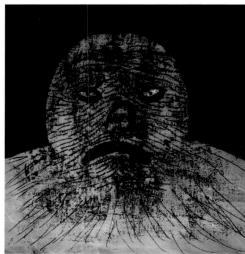

New Talent Refresh! Award • Silver

Sponsored by The Coningsby Gallery

Rachel Louise
Circus Sideshows: Fat Folk

College University Of Derby
Medium Collage
Brief Create a set of sequential illustrations based around the title 'Circus'.
Course Visual Communication: Illustration
Course leader Tracy Tomlinson

Rachel Louise comes from a little village in the suburbs of Nottingham. She's a Visual Communication student at the University of Derby who is getting ready to enter the big wide world of work!

She loves to combine drawing with collage and enjoys experimenting with new ways of doing this, as well as creating characters and thinking about the different ways of describing the human form.

Rachel always has a sketchbook and pen in her bag. Her surroundings and family inspire her and she constantly takes photographs. She is forever looking for unusual, objects and patterns to use in her illustrations.

New Talent Refresh! Award • Bronze
Sponsored by The Coningsby Gallery

Christopher Knight
A Blue Day

College University of Lincoln
Medium Digital and mixed media
Brief Self Initiated Project: A Blue Day is one of a
series of illustrations that respond to words and
phrases. The collection of work is intended to be
viewed as a journal of visual ideas.
Course BA Hons Illustration
Course leader Howard Pemberton

Christopher Knight grew up on the
Welsh border climbing trees, drawing
imaginary creatures and creating
LEGO worlds.

The foundation course at Hereford
College of Arts allowed Christopher
to explore his passion for sequential
images. After experimenting in
drawing, printmaking and animation
he earned a distinction and a place on
Lincoln University's BA Hons
Illustration course.

Studying at Lincoln enabled
Christopher to explore contemporary
illustration. During his studies he
became interested in how words and
images can enhance, manipulate or
contradict one another.

Influenced by adult literature,
contemporary picture books, animation
and folk music, Christopher will
graduate in the summer of 2011.

NEW TALENT

Each entry is marked by the jury
according to how well the work fulfils
the brief, originality, and technical
ability. Only the highest scoring images
are invited to feature in the annual.

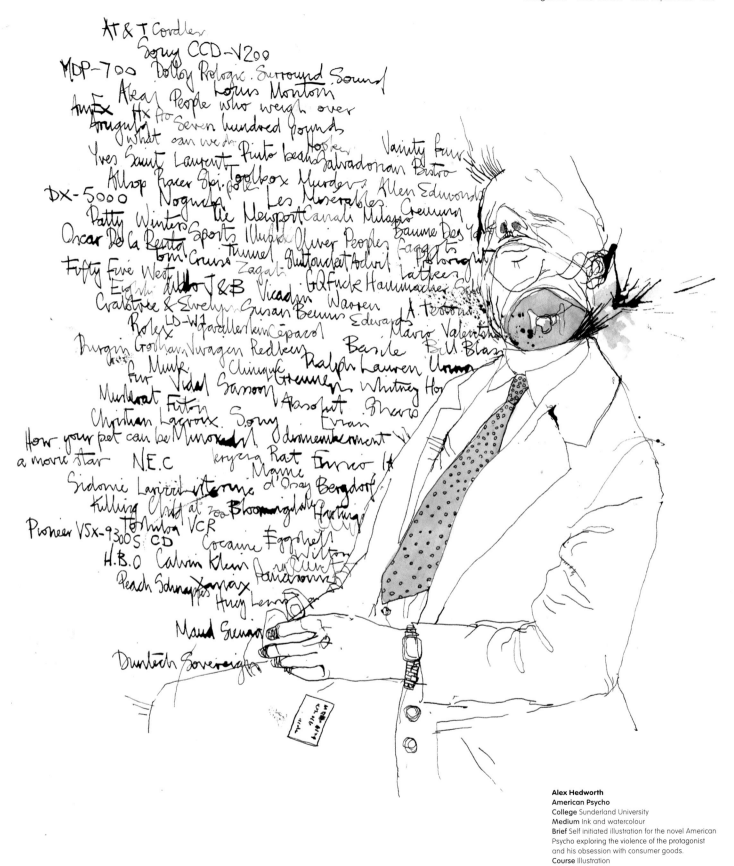

Alex Hedworth
American Psycho
College Sunderland University
Medium Ink and watercolour
Brief Self initiated illustration for the novel American Psycho exploring the violence of the protagonist and his obsession with consumer goods.
Course Illustration
Course Leader Alison Barratt

Madalina Andronic
The Beldam
College Camberwell College of Arts
Medium Watercolour, colored pencils and ink
Brief The real life of the characters from the Romanian folk fairytales: The Beldam (known for hating and abusing children in fairytales; here, during her real-life job as a baby-sitter).
Course MA Illustration
Course Leader Janet Woolley

How-To-Lose-A-Hero-In-10-Days
College Camberwell College of Arts
Medium Watercolour, colored pencils and ink
Brief The real life of the characters from the Romanian folk fairytales: The-Dragon-of-all-Dragons (while documentig about fighting techniques and disincentives to eliminate Prince Charming once and for all).
Course MA Illustration
Course Leader Janet Woolley

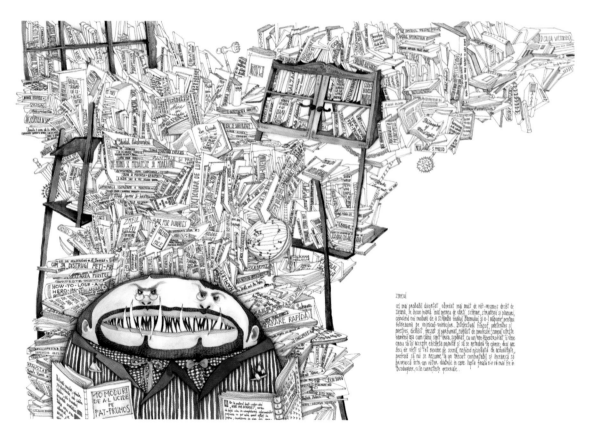

Anna Suwalowska
"Black Poison"
College Camberwell College of Arts
Medium Mixed media
Brief The illustration shows the problem of
human depression inflicted by the outer world.
Course BA Hons Illustration
Course Leader Darryl Clifton

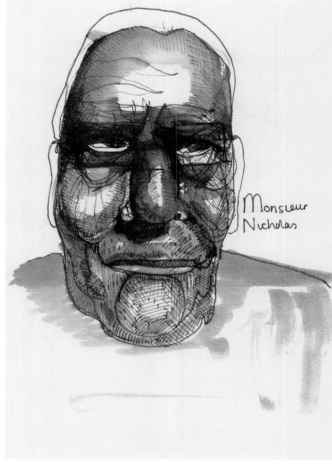

Monsieur
Nicholas

Oliver Butcher
Swimmers
College University of Plymouth
Medium Gouache
Brief A series of designs illustrating sporting
events. Usage suitable for wall murals.
Course BA Hons Illustration
Course Leader Ashley Potter

Helen Butler
Monser
College University of Plymouth
Medium Ink
Brief Depict the main characters in Paul Gallico's
'Love of Seven Dolls' for use as internal illustrations.
Course BA Hons Illustration
Course Leader Ashley Potter

Laura Kingdon
Meavy
College University of Plymouth
Medium Mixed media
Brief Produce a series of images
cataloguing the rural village of Meavy.
Course BA Hons Illustration
Course Leader Ashley Potter

Sam Rennocks
Little Oak
College University of Plymouth
Medium Digital and mixed media
Brief A poster which is an
amalgam of individual cards
illustrating the development of
an American Indian. Each card
contains historical and cultural
facts referred to on the verso.
Course BA Hons Illustration
Course Leader Ashley Potter

Andrew Lester
Mr Portsmouth
College Sheffield Hallam
Medium Ink
Brief Portsmouth's Biggest Fan - John
Portsmouth Football Club Westwood
(changed by deed poll) explains how his
real passion is actually books.
Course Graphic Design
Course Leader Pam Bowman

The Great Wall Of Blackpool
College Sheffield Hallam
Medium Ink
Brief Does Blackpool Really Deserve to
Become a World Heritage Site? Stonehenge,
Wall of China... Blackpool? Visualise this.
Course Graphic Design
Course Leader Pam Bowman

Frances Moffatt
Sunglasses Girl
College Teesside University
Medium Digital and mixed media
Brief Fashion illustration for Spring/Summer
season promotional postcard.
Course MA Future Design
Course Leader Barbara Usherwood

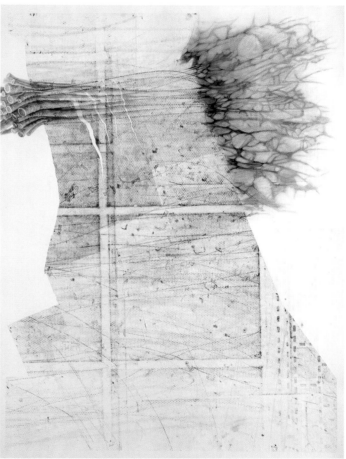

Mirinae Chang
After The Rainy Windy Day
College Central Saint Martins College of Art and Design
Medium Red coloured carbon paper with watercolour,
coloured pencil and pastel
Brief Searching for invisible forms of the realm of
unawareness. Carbon paper sheets were laid on streets
where cars and pedestrians could pass on them. On top
of the marks created, drawings were added.
Course MA Communication Design, Illustration
Course Leader Andrew Foster

By The Waitrose Supermarket, Finchley Road
College Central Saint Martins College of Art and Design
Medium Blue coloured carbon paper with watercolour,
conte, charcoal and coloured pencil
Brief Carbon paper sheets were laid by the exit doors of
Waitrose supermarket to gain unexpected marks from
shopping carts and baby buggies. Then associated
drawings were added on top of the marks created.
Course MA Communication Design, Illustration
Course Leader Andrew Foster

Polly Horne
Three Men In A Boat
College Southampton Solent University
Medium Paper cut-out with hand-painted paper
and pen and ink drawing
Brief Book Cover Design For 'Three Men In A Boat'
By Jerome K. Jerome. This piece was the outcome
of my final project at University. The aim was to
modernise and update a classic novel in order to
make it appeal more to modern day readers.
Course Illustration
Course Leader Peter Lloyd

Hazel Critchley
Maybe We Can Hide Here
College University of Huddersfield
Medium Acetate and pencil
Brief Illustrating 10 fictional facts. Some true and
some made up, so obscure that it would be hard to
tell fact from fiction. This image illustrates the myth
that ostriches bury their heads in the ground.
Course Communication Design Illustration
Course Leader Brent Hardy-Smith

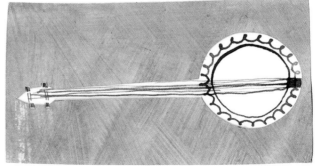

Anna Gibson
For All You Know, I Could Be Pregnant
College Middlesex University
Medium Screenprint
Brief This image is the starting point for an investigation into the nature of overheard conversations. It was supported in Anna's show by a number of smaller prints illustrating specific quotes.
Course BA Hons Illustration
Course Leader Nancy Slonims

James Steadman
Twenty Thousand Leagues Under The Sea
College Middlesex University
Medium Ink
Brief To produce a book cover for Jules Verne's Twenty Thousand Leagues Under The Sea, for a new edition published by Penguin Classics.
Course BA Hons Illustration
Course Leader Nancy Slonims

James Oses
London Guildhall
College Middlesex University
Medium Ink
Brief Part of a reportage project to picture the great Guildhalls, trade buildings and markets of the City of London.
Course BA Hons Illustration
Course Leader Nancy Slonims

Vintners Hall
College Middlesex University
Medium Ink
Brief Part of a reportage project to picture the great Guildhalls, trade buildings and markets of the City of London.
Course BA Hons Illustration
Course Leader Nancy Slonims

Bob Wright
A Room Booked In The Name Of Jamieson
College Middlesex University
Medium Pencil
Brief Spread from a graphic novel adaptation
of J G Ballard's short story "A Gentle Assassin".
Course BA Hons Illustration
Course Leader Nancy Slonims

Adam Cruft
Freddy Morris
College Middlesex University
Medium Etching with aquatint
Brief Produced for a final major project
documenting the people who live and
work in the print room at Middlesex
University, this etching features Freddy
Morris MAIRCA], a mainstay of the facility.
Course BA Hons Illustration
Course Leader Nancy Slonims

«

Niki Neocleous
The Village Of Lefkara
College Middlesex University
Medium Ink
Brief A self initiated project to produce an image
capturing the decorative essence of Lefkara, a
village on the island of Cyprus famous for its
lace, and silver handicrafts.
Course BA Hons Illustration
Course Leader Nancy Slonims

Holly Exley
Jack Black Dreams
College Middlesex University
Medium Watercolour
Brief A spread from an illustrated edition of
Under Milk Wood, a 1954 play by Dylan Thomas.
Course BA Hons Illustration
Course Leader Nancy Slonims

Captin Cat
College Middlesex University
Medium Watercolour
Brief A spread from an illustrated edition of
Under Milk Wood, a 1954 play by Dylan Thomas.
Course BA Hons Illustration
Course Leader Nancy Slonims

Laura Slinn
Bee Girl
College Middlesex University
Medium Ink
Brief A self initiated project, Laura's Bee Girl
became this year's poster girl for illustration
at Middlesex University, and a big selling
postcard in the students' print shop.
Course BA Hons Illustration
Course Leader Nancy Slonims

Holly Trill
Severed Hand
College Middlesex University
Medium Screenprint
Brief A large screenprint produced
to illustrate the 1979 Angela Carter
werewolf tale, The Bloody Chamber.
Course BA Hons Illustration
Course Leader Nancy Slonims

Beetle Wallpaper
College Middlesex University
Medium Screenprint
Brief To take inspiration from the Hunterian Museum's
extensive collection of natural history specimens to produce a
range of hand printed wallpapers for sale in the gallery shop.
Course BA Hons Illustration
Course Leader Nancy Slonims

⌃

Hannah Clark
Kipps
College Middlesex University
Medium Watercolour
Brief To produce an illustrated book cover for Kipps, a novel by H. G. Wells, first published in 1905. This is a wraparound cover featuring the front, spine and back.
Course BA Hons Illustration
Course Leader Nancy Slonims

⌐

4 Cheyne Walk, Chelsea.
College Middlesex University
Medium Watercolour
Brief One of a series of reportage drawings capturing the homes of writers in residential London, this image is a portrait of George Eliot's home in her later years.
Course BA Hons Illustration
Course Leader Nancy Slonims

∧
Dorota Gaweda
Gdansk
College Middlesex University
Medium Pencil
Brief An illustration for the Tin Drum by Günter Grass. This is one of a series of interlinked images which tell parts of the story in a fold-out book format which includes an animated film.
Course BA Hons Illustration
Course Leader Nancy Slonims

〉
Oskar
College Middlesex University
Medium Pencil
Brief An illustration for the Tin Drum by Günter Grass. This is one of a series of interlinked images which tell parts of the story in a fold-out book format which includes an animated film.
Course BA Hons Illustration
Course Leader Nancy Slonims

<
Adam Doyle
It's A Man's World
College Middlesex University
Medium Digital and mixed media
Brief A large poster displaying the configuration
of Adam's mind, this image was the centrepiece
of his show at the Truman Brewery.
Course BA Hons Illustration
Course Leader Nancy Slonims

Claire Jade Minchinton
The Elves
College Coventry University
Medium Collage
Brief To create a series of Illustrations for the
Brothers Grimm classic 'The Elves and the
Shoemaker'. The illustrations are for a 32 page
children's picture book.
Course BA Hons Graphic Design and Illustration
Course Leader Andrew Spackman

Carly Gledhill
Home Sweet House Plant
College University of Central Lancashire
Medium Pencil and marker
Brief As a continuation of work for my Children's book illustration MA this piece takes an every day object, the house plant, and brings to life a fantastical world.
Course MA Children's Book illustration
Course Leader Stephen Wilkin

Eileen-Marie Emerson
Free
College University of Ulster
Medium Digital and mixed media
Brief Children's illustrated picture book
depicting a new mythical tale (from County
Antrim, Northern Ireland) about the forest
here and the enchanted world hidden within.
Course MDes Design Communication
Course Leader Patrick McLaughlin

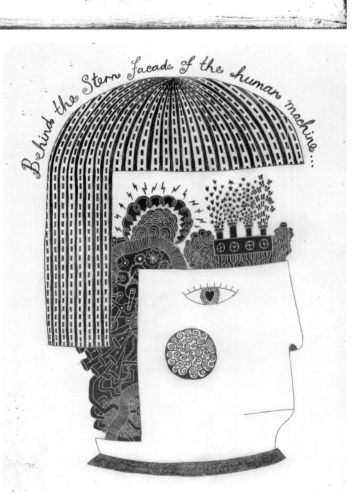

James Grover
Resistance
College University of Lincoln
Medium Digital and mixed media
Brief To create an image which captures
the theme of resistance. The image has to
be effective when reproduced at A2 size.
Course BA Illustration
Course Leader Howard Pemberton

Human Machine
College University of Lincoln
Medium Digital and mixed media
Brief Part of a series of self-promotion
postcards inspired by T.S. Eliot's poem, 'The
Waste Land'. The images are intended to
detail in an eye-catching way what goes
on underneath a 'human machine'.
Course BA Illustration
Course Leader Howard Pemberton

Amy Abbott
Loneliness
College Camberwell College of Arts
Medium Gouache and charcoal
Brief Social Investigation into
women as domestic beings,
influenced by feminist quote
"Loneliness is never more cruel
than when it is felt in close
propinquity with someone who
has ceased to communicate".
Course MA Illustration
Course Leader Janet Woolley

‹
Martha Zmpounou
Anima
College Central Saint Martins College of Art and Design
Medium Ink and pencil on paper
Brief This work is inspired by the Jungian 'Shadow'
archetype, a part of the unconscious mind which consists
of our hidden weaknesses and repressed instincts.
Course MA Communication Design - Illustration
Course Leader Andrew Foster

Thomas Legge
Train From The Landlady Series
College University for the Creative Arts
Medium Photo-etching
Brief This image is based on the story by
Roald Dahl entitled the Landlady, from my
final major project. This is the first picture
when the train pulls into the station.
Course BA Hons Illustration
Course Leader Neil Breeden

Sector 4 Illustration
Nothing Gets Crossed Out
College UCLAN
Medium Brush & Ink and Digital Media
Brief To illustrate a book of quotes on entering
and working in the creative industry from current
professionals to new graduates and students.
Course BA Hons Illustration
Course Leader Steven Wilkin

Golbanou Moghaddas
A Place For My Heart
College Central Saint Martins
College of Art & Design
Medium Etching
Brief My project is about the journey of
a feminine spirit who is questioning her
existence and trying to deal with her
emotions on the way to find tranquility
and love in her life.
Course Communication Design, Illustration
Course Leader Andrew Foster

Do You Fancy A Cup Of Tea In My Heart?
College Central Saint Martins
College of Art & Design
Medium Etching
Brief My project is about the journey of
a feminine spirit who is questioning her
existence and trying to deal with her
emotions on the way to find tranquility
and love in her life.
Course Communication Design, Illustration
Course Leader Andrew Foster

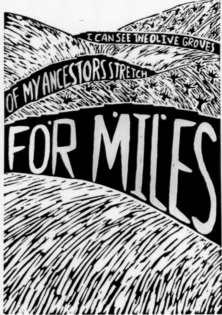

Emma Carpendale
Amy And The Origami Man
College University of Northampton
Medium Digital and mixed media
Brief This book was my Final Major Project. It is a children's picture book that has a central theme of friendship and deals with the issues of loneliness and fears and how to overcome them.
Course BA Illustration
Course Leader John Holt

Amy And The Origami Man Front Cover
College University of Northampton
Medium Digital and mixed media
Brief This book was my Final Major Project. It is a children's picture book that has a central theme of friendship and deals with the issues of loneliness and fears and how to overcome them.
Course BA Illustration
Course Leader John Holt

Ellie Wintram
The Wall
College Central Saint Martins
Medium Linoprint
Brief My ironic thoughts from visits to the Israel/West Bank divide convey the wall's devastating effect on Palestinian life through its scale, restriction and surveillance.
Course BA Hons Graphic Design and Illustration
Course Leader Andrew Hall

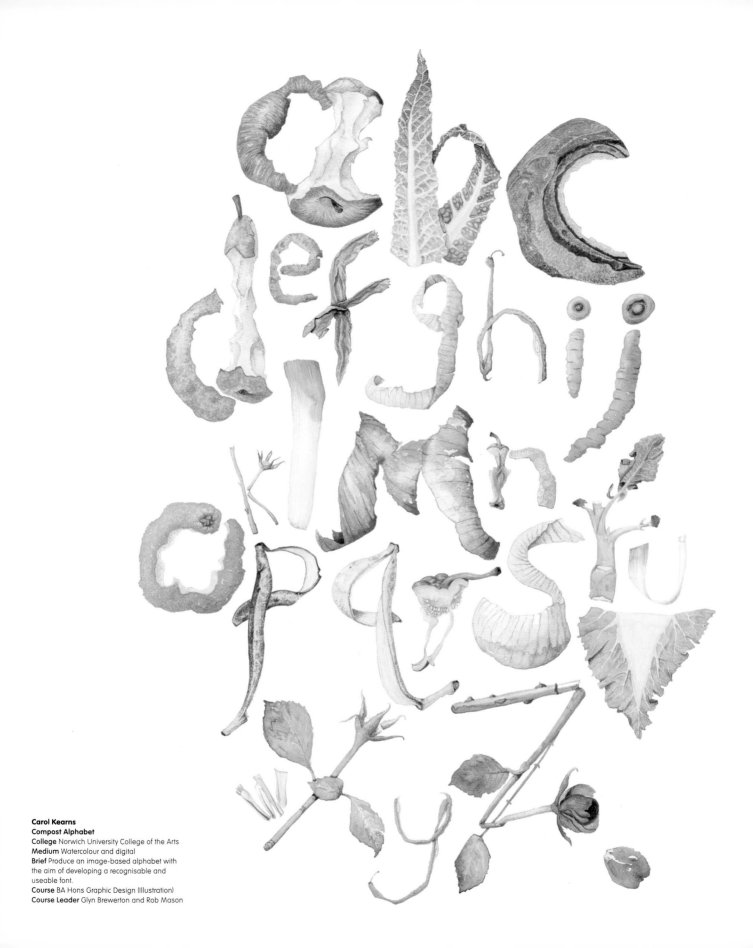

Carol Kearns
Compost Alphabet
College Norwich University College of the Arts
Medium Watercolour and digital
Brief Produce an image-based alphabet with
the aim of developing a recognisable and
useable font.
Course BA Hons Graphic Design (Illustration)
Course Leader Glyn Brewerton and Rob Mason

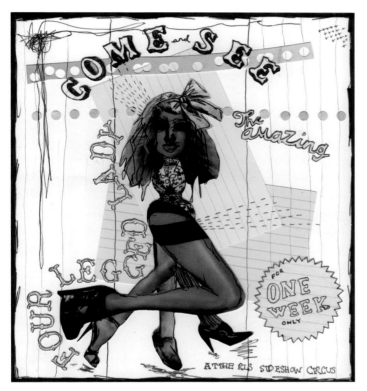

Rachel Louise
Circus Sideshow: Four Legged Lady
College University of Derby
Medium Collage
Brief Create a set of sequential illustrations based around the title 'Circus'.
Course Visual Communication: Illustration
Course Leader Tracy Tomlinson

Circus Sideshow: Armless Woman
College University of Derby
Medium Collage
Brief Create a set of sequential illustrations based around the title 'Circus'.
Course Visual Communication: Illustration
Course Leader Tracy Tomlinson

In desperation, Sam reached into his pockets and threw all of the bits and bobs and leaves and shells he had, until his pockets were empty.

And with every object that he threw, the Barrodor slowed and stumbled, slowed and curled and shrunk... down and down and down....

Leaving nothing but a pile of pearls upon the floor.

Emma Reynolds
The Barrodor Chase
College Manchester School of Art
Medium Mixed media
Brief Illustration from 'The Barrodor', an original fairy tale that can also be read as a story about loneliness and isolation, the need for companionship, and overcoming our personal demons.
Course Illustration with Animation
Course Leader Ian McCullough

Mike Schofield
Rent
College University of Lincoln
Medium Acrylic
Brief Part of a self-negotiated project entitled 'strange places', intended to reflect the surprising and unexpected nature of discovering new cultures.
Course Illustration
Course Leader Alec Shepley

Louise Rouse
Grooming
College Tama Art University
Medium Digital and mixed media
Brief To illustrate how man interacts with his environment, and the changed relationship between man and nature in Japan.
Course MA Illustration
Course Leader Takashi Akiyama

2020 Ginza Old New Bricktown
College Tama Art University
Medium Digital and mixed media
Brief Ginza was the birthplace of modernity in Japan, associated with high fashion since the 1900s. Now, apiarists are turning it into an oasis for honeybees and urban agriculture. Depicting this makeover.
Course MA Illustration
Course Leader Takashi Akiyama

1.September 1939
I am 14, doing well at school, but the beginning of the war destroys all the hope of other studies. I help my parents at home.

17 September 1939
War with Germany enters its third week. Stalin helps Hitler; the Soviet Union invades Poland. The Red Army occupies our village.

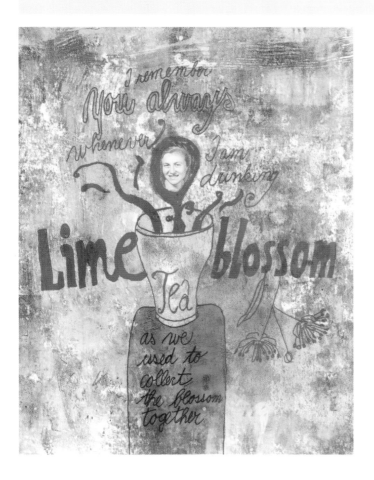

Marketa Lukasova
The Washing Line
College University of Derby
Medium Digital and mixed media
Brief UnOrdinary Life - an imaginative diary revealing my grandmother's secret that changed and altered the journey of her life.
Course Graphic Design
Course Leader Tracy Tomlinson

Lime Blossom
College University of Derby
Medium Digital and mixed media
Brief UnOrdinary Life - I remember my grandmother always whenever I am drinking lime blossom tea.
Course Graphic Design
Course Leader Tracy Tomlinson

Petra Kneile
'Her Face Was A Painted Mask Of Beauty.'
Angela Carter
College Camberwell College of Arts
Medium Digital and mixed media
Brief This image is part of my MA Illustration
project, exploring the representation of
self and the expression of identity through
appearance and dress.
Course MA Illustration (Visual Arts)
Course Leader Janet Woolley

Paul Scheruebel
Jealousy
College University of Westminster
Medium Oil
Brief Produce a piece of work that deals, in the
broadest sense, with the title "a recipe for disaster".
Course BA Hons Illustration
Course Leader Liz Grob

Index

Index

Index

Acknowledgements

The AOI would like to thank:
All members of the jury for applying their expertise to the difficult task of selecting the best of all the entries now published in this book.

As always, Sabine Reimer, Images Co-ordinator, for her efficiency and cheerful dedication during the production of Images 35.

Special thanks go to Simon Sharville for his creative involvement during the design process.

Victoria Topping, whose image "Cockerel" was used to promote the Images 35 Call For Entries.

Images 35 could not have been organised without the help of our dedicated casual staff and volunteers and we are very grateful for their invaluable assistance.

Last but not least, we are grateful for the support of the many organisations and individuals who contribute to the success of the Images exhibition and annual by submitting their work for others to judge.

The AOI Board and staff

About the AOI

The Association of Illustrators was established in 1973 to advance and protect illustrators' rights. It is a non-profit making trade association dedicated to its members' professional interests and the promotion of contemporary illustration. As the only body to represent illustrators and campaign for their rights in the UK, the AOI has successfully increased the standing of illustration as a profession and improved the commercial and ethical conditions of employment for illustrators. On behalf of its members and with their continued support, the AOI can achieve goals that it would be difficult or impossible for creators to attempt alone.

A voice for illustration
The AOI provides a voice for professional illustrators and by weight of numbers and expertise is able to work at enforcing the rights of freelance illustrators at every stage of their careers. AOI liaises with national and international organisations, agents and illustrators over industry problems and campaigns against unfair contracts and terms of trade.

Campaigning
The AOI was responsible for establishing the right for illustrators to retain ownership of their artwork and helped to establish the secondary rights arm of the Designers and Artists Copyright Society (DACS), the UK visual arts collecting society. In addition, it lobbies parliament for better legislation for illustrators through the British Copyright Council (BCC) and the Creators Rights Alliance (CRA). During 2011 AOI submitted responses to government reviews on copyright, to ensure that the views of illustrators are represented. The AOI is also a founder member of the European Illustrators Forum (EIF), a network established to create a stronger force for illustration within Europe.

Pro-Action: Visual Artist In Business
The Pro-Action committee was established by the AOI and the Society of Artists Agents to deal with the problems facing commercial artists in today's market place. The aims of the group are to tackle fee erosion, increasingly detrimental contract terms from clients and to campaign for visual artists' rights.

The Association of Photographers and the Professional Cartoonists Organisation joined the group in 2010. For further information please visit pro-action.org.uk

Information and Support Services
AOI continues to provide invaluable services to its members, and ensures they are kept up to date with relevant industry information. Members of the AOI not only sustain campaigning and networking to improve working conditions for all, they benefit personally from AOI services. Members stay informed with our wide range of events and seminars.

Varoom magazine and the twicemonthly 'UPmail' email newsletter keep members up to date with events, practice and developments in the industry. Members receive up to 50% off our topical range of events and forums, themes ranging from children's books, to self-promotion, business planning and up-to-the-minute industry debates.

Resources to help illustrators succeed
Members receive large discounts on essential publications, including the Images annual, The Illustrator's Guide to Law and Business Practice and our range of targeted directory listings of illustration commissioners. Members of the AOI receive discounts in art shops around the country.

Resources to help commissioners succeed
The AOI's Guide to Commissioning Illustration saves time and money by guiding AOI member commissioners safely through the pitfalls of the commissioning process. Selected commissioners receive Images, the definitive jury-selected Illustration source book in the UK, free of charge. Our online portfolios at AOIportfolios. com give commissioners looking for the perfect artist for their projects access to more than 15000 classified images and the creator's contact details in an instant.

Essential professional and business advice
Members have access to a free dedicated hotline for legal, ethical and pricing advice, discounted consultations with our industry specialists including a chartered accountant and the UK's premier portfolio consultant.

Promotion
AOI members receive substantial discounts on the AOI's online portfolios at AOIportfolios.com and the Images competition, annual and exhibition, showcasing the best of British contemporary illustration. The annual is despatched to over 4000 prominent commissioners of illustration in the UK and overseas. All information on Images can be found at AOIimages.com

Inspiration
AOI regularly organizes talks with leading illustrators, industry debates and offers its members discounted entry to competitions and exhibitions. Members receive a free subscription to Varoom magazine - a rich celebration of illustration and its role within culture and society. The magazine features interviews with leading illustrators and image-makers as well as in-depth articles on different aspects and themes of contemporary illustration. Its stimulating line-up of interviews, profiles, history and polemic make Varoom essential reading for everyone interested in visual communication. See more at varoomlab.com

Contact
To request further information or a membership application form please telephone +44 (0)20 7613 4328 or email info@theaoi.com

Website
Visit the AOI's website at theAOI.com for details of the Association's activities, details of forthcoming events and online tickets, listings and reviews, the AOI's history, and to purchase publications or view online portfolios.

Association of illustrators

theAOI.com

Publications

The illustrator's Guide to Law and Business Practice

This comprehensive manual covers all aspects of the law likely to affect illustrators. It contains recommended terms and conditions, advice on calculating fees, how to write a licence agreement and be protected against exploitative practices. Interspersed with contemporary illustrations, the handbook was written by Simon Stern, a renowned expert on illustration and the law, and is the result of many years of research. It has been approved by intellectual property experts, law firm Finers Stephens Innocent.

Client directories

AOI produce three essential Directories. The Publishing Directory lists circa 170, and the Editorial Directory more than 280 illustration clients with full contact details; the Advertising Directory holds details of about 150 advertising agencies who commission illustration – providing an invaluable source of information for all practitioners. Each directory includes notes of what kind of illustration is published by the client and we update and add contact details to each list every year. CD ROMs are also supplied with addresses and preformatted labels for printing.

Varoom – illustration, culture, society

Varoom is devoted to exploring the world of illustration and image-making. The magazine looks at practitioners from around the world who are making significant contributions to the constantly evolving art of illustration, on both a commercial and culturally significant level. Varoom provides writers, commentators, academics and illustrators with a platform from which to take a critical yet accessible look at trends and developments in the illustrated image.

Published three times a year, available on subscription and in specialist bookshops in the UK and worldwide, free to members.

The Varoom website has information on current and back issues, and features web-only content, reviews and articles. varoomlab.com

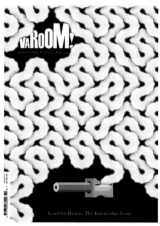

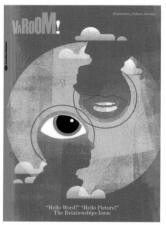

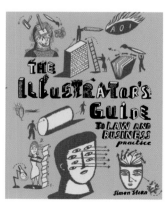

Information

Report on illustration fees and standards of pricing

This informative report was revised in April 2007 and can be found in the members section of the AOI website. It contains information from an online survey, AOI data collated over many years and invaluable contributions from agents, art buyers and selected working professionals. Properly researched costing and pricing structures is a central plank in maintaining business viability, and illustrators should consider the true cost of their services when determining rates. AOI believes this report builds awareness of the importance of carefully considered pricing for both illustrators and commissioners.

UPmail email newsletter

UPmail, published twice monthly, brings you the latest industry news, AOI events information, campaigns, initiatives and listings of relevant exhibitions and publications.
To subscribe, visit the News section on the AOI website.

theAOI.com - illustration resources for commissioners and practitioners

Visit the website for details on AOI membership and the Association's activities, including UPmail e-newsletter, details of forthcoming events and campaigns, the AOI's history, news and reviews, and to purchase publications and tickets. The Members Only section contains exclusive articles and reviews and the AOI Pricing Survey.

To order publications online go to theAOI.com
To subscribe to Varoom go to varoomlab.com
For further information please contact the Association of Illustrators on +44 (0)20 7613 4328
or email info@theaoi.com.

theAOI.com

AOI Portfolios

Scott Gwilliams
Canada

Steve Simpson
Ireland

Brian Fitzgerald
Ireland

Annebritt Ullén
Sweden

Daniel Pudles
Belgium

Naja Conrad-Hansen
Denmark

Evgenia Beljaeva
Germany

Sam Vinhyl
France

Heather Wyville
USA

Valeria Petrone
Italy

Steven Noble
USA

justin sola
Spain

Noumeda Carbone
Italy

Lorenzo Sabbatini
Italy

Natalie Brockett
Japan

Lio Beardsley
Hong Kong

Justine Beckett
New Zealand

Elizabeth Barnett
Australia

Greg Holt
Australia

Niki Leonidou
Greece

Some of our international friends

180,000 unique visitors per year

AOIportfolios.com